Intentionallies(abb. ITL)
1 (adj) unknown, unseen, untouched etc.
2 (adj) (sometimes) smooth but edgy / contemporary / everchanging
3 (v) (used as a slang) to create something intentionally

Clearly, to me, it is necessary to recognize the zeitgeist and then, in that instant, to place myself at the core of current consciousness.

Autumn 1995
Intentionallies was established in 1995 as a firm dedicated to realizing architecture and design through convincing ideas and fine craftsmanship. The projects Intentionallies have undertaken span a broad spectrum and are unified by the depth to which each concept is considered. The firm embraces the unusual, and in doing so, has become a pioneer. Whether crafting a piece of furniture or the tallest of high-rise buildings, Intentionallies is not bound by convention.

Intentionallies in the 21st Century
The words that buzz about the office are 'future classics', 'quick thinking', 'stereoscopic views of tasks', 'integration of ideas', 'assembly of fragments', and 'alliances'. These ideas epitomize what Intentionallies is about.

Tradition is something to which inventive ideas are added and then passed down over time. Tradition evolves, reflecting the tastes and forms of the time. You cannot let original forms dominate you without understanding the reasons for them.

Architecture, for us, is about striving to create future classics. Specialization has resulted in projects being divided among product designers, interior designers, landscape designers, and architects. Although this is a reasonable solution, professionals seem to have lost the ability to turn their hands to working in a broader field. What Intentionallies aims for is not division, but harmony, where all the elements within a space are achieved by architects, as was done at the beginning of the 20th century.

From the moment Intentionallies was established, our goals have been to be true to the design process and to aggressively take advantage of the almost chemical reaction that occurs when talented professionals from various fields meet, impelling them to explore new concepts. As Intentionallies was founded by three people, we are able to complete projects three times as fast as a firm headed by a single architect, where only one project is realized, on average, every 10 years. While we adhere to our intention of completing a project every three years, we also constantly attempt to reach beyond the targets we've set ourselves. We, at Intentionallies, aim to be a recognizable brand.

Shuwa Tei

in this context

surpass

opportunity

beyond the boundary
of architecture

gravity's rainbow

01. Materiality

In our daily lives, we are surrounded by all types of materials, whether we're conscious of them or not. Intentionallies strives to express the original feel, colour, and form of the materials the firm uses. When designing spaces, Intentionallies believes that the mix and balance of materials is of paramount importance. When creating a space with the warm look of wood, for example, the firm doesn't simply use timber in different applications, but also considers its relationship with other materials, and how a blend will bring out the beauty of the main material. To accomplish this, the special characteristics and appearance of the specific material are taken into account, along with the best type of coating to use to achieve the desired finish. Revealing the essential beauty of a material is, to Intentionallies, materiality.

02. Dealing with Gravity

Craftsmanship through architecture is Intentionallies' creed. The definition of three-dimensional is becoming ever wider and in the future, it may change further still. Shuwa Tei comments, 'To me, three-dimensional means spatialization, which starts with architecture and proceeds on through everything else.' He continues, 'When I first started studying architecture, I felt that in the main, what I was studying referred to structures. We eventually designed a building, but I strongly felt that I had to explore and experiment more first.' investigating the visual and emotional impact of inflatable structures, Intentionallies used balloons to play with gravity, making, as ever, an honest connection between different elements.

03. At Home in Tokyo

'I've learnt a great deal about Tokyo just by living in the city,' says Shuwa Tei. 'That is why I felt compelled to found Intentionallies here in Tokyo.' He continues, 'It's vital not to be separated from the city. Living in Tokyo has led me to believe that it is important to be able to constantly define our relationships with society. We need to equip ourselves with the capacity to make definitive judgments about the urban landscape. At Intentionallies we focus on what the word "home" means to us, what it means in architecture, and we strive to create the spaces that we've been dreaming of.'

04. The Beauty of Japan

One aspect of design is taking ancient traditions and techniques and reinventing them, giving them a new value. Shuwa Tei explains, 'It's creating meaning anew. Traditions must evolve. Linking state-of-the-art technology to the newest developments must be made a priority. Continuity then has the possibility of becoming a tradition in the future, of becoming a classic.' Tei continues, 'I have taken the industrial art of the 20th century and reinterpreted it with today's sense of beauty, expressing it in terms of today's Japan. I have been inspired by objects and events from history and woven them into objects and spaces we've designed. Although a standard design language exists, and is used throughout the world, I consider traditional beauty and an appreciation of the four seasons a vital component to design.'

05. The Architecture of Space / Atmosphere

What is meant by the description stylishly dignified? Shuwa Tei comments, 'I often think about this. It is not something that can be attributed to history, status, value, reputation or genre. It transcends drawings and computer graphics. It is quite simply intrinsic to a space, one that feels fresh and new but is nonetheless comforting. The way materials and furnishings are handled plays a vital role in the overall stylishly dignified nature of a space.

Architecture and interiors are anchored in their location. We consider the relationship between a site and its culture, history and the context of the location to be of the utmost importance. When devising a solution, we continually search for that elusive, stylishly dignified quality as we shape the atmosphere, wrapping each space in subtle, delicate details while erasing all traces of our labour to ensure the result is effortless.'

06. Communication / Collaboration

In demonstrating concepts for a building design, for either the exterior or the interior, it is impractical to show it full scale. Shuwa Tei elaborates, saying, 'If you could, that would be ideal. You can, however, use models, two-dimensional graphics or design sketches, but there is definitely a gap between those and the real thing. In using these techniques there is scope for the views of colleagues to be considered. It is not a question of right or wrong; sometimes we complete the design, sometimes we leave parts blank. We are particularly conscious at this stage that we are communicating with each other, therefore we don't rely on established means, rather, we are constantly searching for new methods of communication.'

Tei continues, 'Intentionallies starts from the premise that, while something can be planned and designed by one person, it cannot be made by one person, but we do not stop there. We believe that it is very beneficial to collaborate enthusiastically to learn new things of new value. This collaboration involves not only graphic designers, web designers and artists but it also extends to craftsmen who have traditional knowledge and skills, learned scholars from other fields, research facilities with specialized technologies, talented engineers and other professionals. Our objective is to constantly aim for the optimum solution and to produce something of the highest value. There are no rules or established methods for achieving this: we always approach a problem with an open mind and with determination to find the best possible solution.'

07. Solution / Standpoint

Shuwa Tei says, 'Many projects begin with a request from the client; we ask ourselves: what is the problem to be solved? First we consider the aim of the client, then we establish the target to be achieved, all the while sharing our thoughts with the client. We do not look for answers by merely looking at our past work and reusing old solutions: we always take a fresh look and search for the best answer. It is important to us to convey our unique style to the client. In this way, we feel that we can share our goals with our client.

It has always been our aim and practice to act spontaneously and be the source of original ideas. In one scheme, for Hanamidzuki in 1999, we became entrepreneurs and established a restaurant that was to be the inspiration for the entire programme. We tried our hands at something quite new. We took on not just the design but also the responsibilities of management, learning about the service industry, including the provision of food and the areas for cooking and eating, while always looking at the design from the point of view of both workers and customers. In doing this we found a variety of fundamental concepts. There are times when we feel that it is important to change our standpoint. This is how our partnership with the consumer electronics brand, amadana, started in 2002. We recognized that it was important first to create a parent company that would establish the principles of the design. On the basis of this rationale, we established a consumer electronics joint venture with our partner. This encouraged us to create a viable system in which we could profit and also take part in decision making.'

08. The Evolution of Design Fashioned by Time

Shuwa Tei begins, 'I have been thinking about the relationship between Tokyo and the rest of the world from the Japanese angle. They say that the apparent distance between Japan and the rest of Asia, and between the East and the West is shrinking but I feel that it is inevitable that Japan's designs are being distilled from its original culture and crystallized with the passage of time. I would like to be able to understand creative inspiration but this cannot be achieved merely by collecting facts. In places where temporal and spatial axes cross like the warp and weft of fabric, I want to create original but inevitable solutions that are the two-way marriage of the interior with the exterior. To continue my acquisition of information I search out different places, finding new opportunities and occasionally creating new forms.'

09. Creating a New Urban Area

Shuwa Tei says, 'The way urban areas are being formed is dramatically different from the past. We can now forecast that circumstances are more unpredictable than ever. Mobile devices have changed the way people relate to their local area and the way they make commitments. Furthermore, dramatic changes have been brought to methods of communication. Methods of work are changing too: a designer no longer sharpens a pencil and sits at a drafting table with tracing paper but instead, faces a computer screen. Much of what once required going physically to a site, modifying a drawing, sharing information, or obtaining data concerning it, can now be done with the click of a mouse. We've always wanted to find our own solution as to how we can instantly make a connection with and commit ourselves to a hectically changing urban environment. In some cities we are exploring the possibility of supplying clean electrical energy throughout by 2010. While we believe that realizing this goal at Haneda Airport may be difficult, we think that it could be done under licence in other cities. I say this with conviction because of our successful experience in facing challenges in many different parts of the globe. This is the world as we see it: exploring consumer electronics is part of the architectural design process. Creating the amadana line from the ground upwards was the first step in our participation in the formation of future urban areas. With this credo we look forward to taking the fullest possible part in the construction of the urban areas of the future.'

W104×D49×H14.5mm

W265,000×D88,250×H166,000mm

For the better part of a decade I've been struck by this recurring fantasy every time I wander the streets of Tokyo. It doesn't matter where I am, the time of day, the people I'm with or even the mood I'm in – at any moment I can easily become lost in a private little fantasy that only happens in Tokyo and never fails to lighten my mood. The trigger for these delightful daydreams can take any form – it can be the whir of a bicycle passing by on a back lane in Meguro, a thicket of bamboo in a tiny garden in Daikanyama or a cosily lit bar glimpsed from a cab while zipping through Aoyama. Scenes as simple and everyday as these are all it takes for me to start imagining what life would be like in Tokyo if I could build it from scratch. While the neighbourhoods for my residence constantly change (Yoyogi Uehara one day and then Ebisu the next), the architect does not.

At about the same time my design-focused daydreams started, I was introduced to architect Shuwa Tei and his firm Intentionallies. We first met in the basement of a small restaurant he designed near Harajuku and the day after we embarked on a tour of other projects he'd designed in and around the area – the highlight being the shop Strasburgo just off of Gaien Nishi-dori. Thereafter I enjoyed frequent meetings with Tei-san and his colleagues and in a certain way he became my unofficial tutor for all things related to Japanese design.

Over the years I've enjoyed tours of Kyoto, been treated to favourite restaurants and introduced to an eclectic and always intriguing mix of people from various industries – all with Tei-san at my side. In many ways, my take on Japan has been very much informed by his guiding eye, candid opinions and thoughtful explanations. At the same time I've also had the great pleasure of working with him on a variety of industrial design, branding and media projects that have proved to be some of the most rewarding of my career.

Intentionallies recently moved into new headquarters in Tokyo's Jingumae district – with offices on the lower levels and Tei's residence on the top floors. The building has now become a reference point for the way I'd like to one day work and live. Meetings are held in a wonderful double height space on the ground floor while days can end with a relaxing bath in a hinoki tub with views across the neighbourhood. I'm hoping we still get to build something together. I think about a small hotel in Harajuku, a perfectly formed apartment project in London, a small resort in a small bay somewhere in Kyushu or perhaps even the perfect transport terminal that the world would want to transit through. If nothing else, I do hope we'll collaborate on building that tiny house of my dreams on a shady Tokyo side street – someday.

Tyler Brûlé

Chairman and Creative Director, Winkreative / Editor in Chief, *Monocle*

INTENTIONALLIES
SHAPING *JAPAN* AND BEYOND

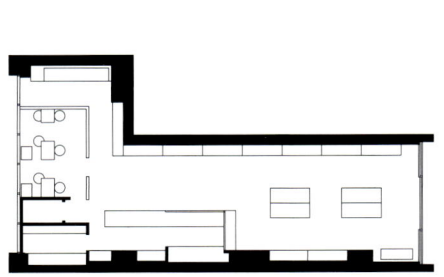
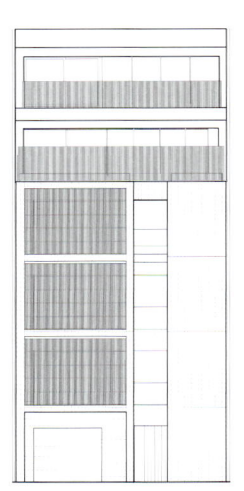
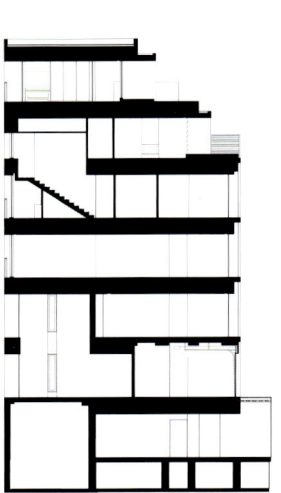
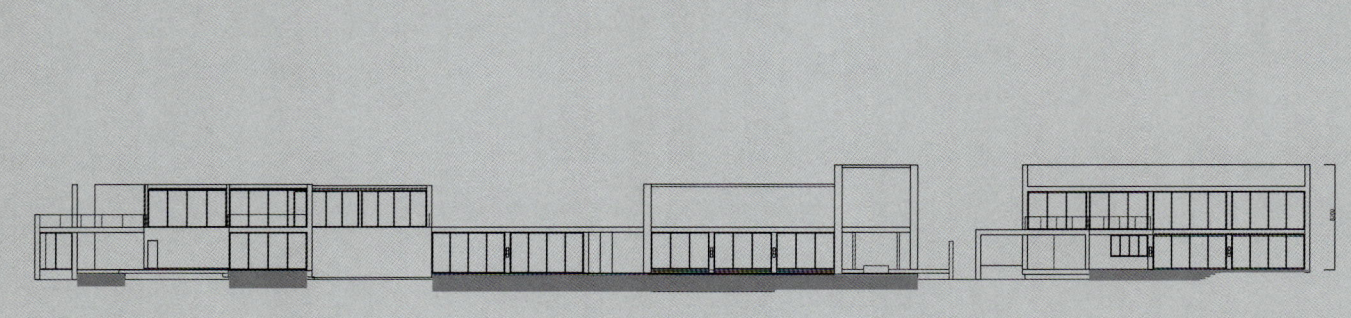

INTENTIONALLIES

Aestrwy td Dewnd the
Defwritien wrem the Architecture.   Fowso to Defend the Meaowsh of
Architecturw

**From furniture to the tallest of high-rise buildings,
its work is notbound by any established frames.**

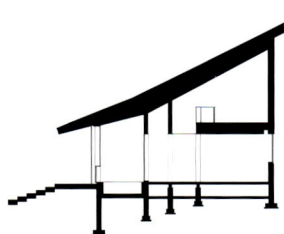 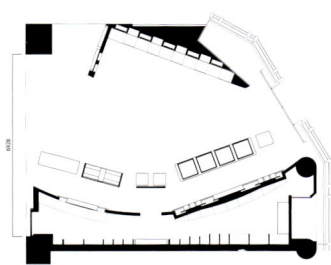 

INTENTIONALLIES

AD — ASSEMBLY TO DESIGN THE DEFINITION WITHIN THE ARCHITECTURE

FD·MFA — FUSION TO DEFINE THE MEANINGS BY ARCHITECTURES

From furniture to the tallest of high-rise buildings, its work is not bound by any established frames.

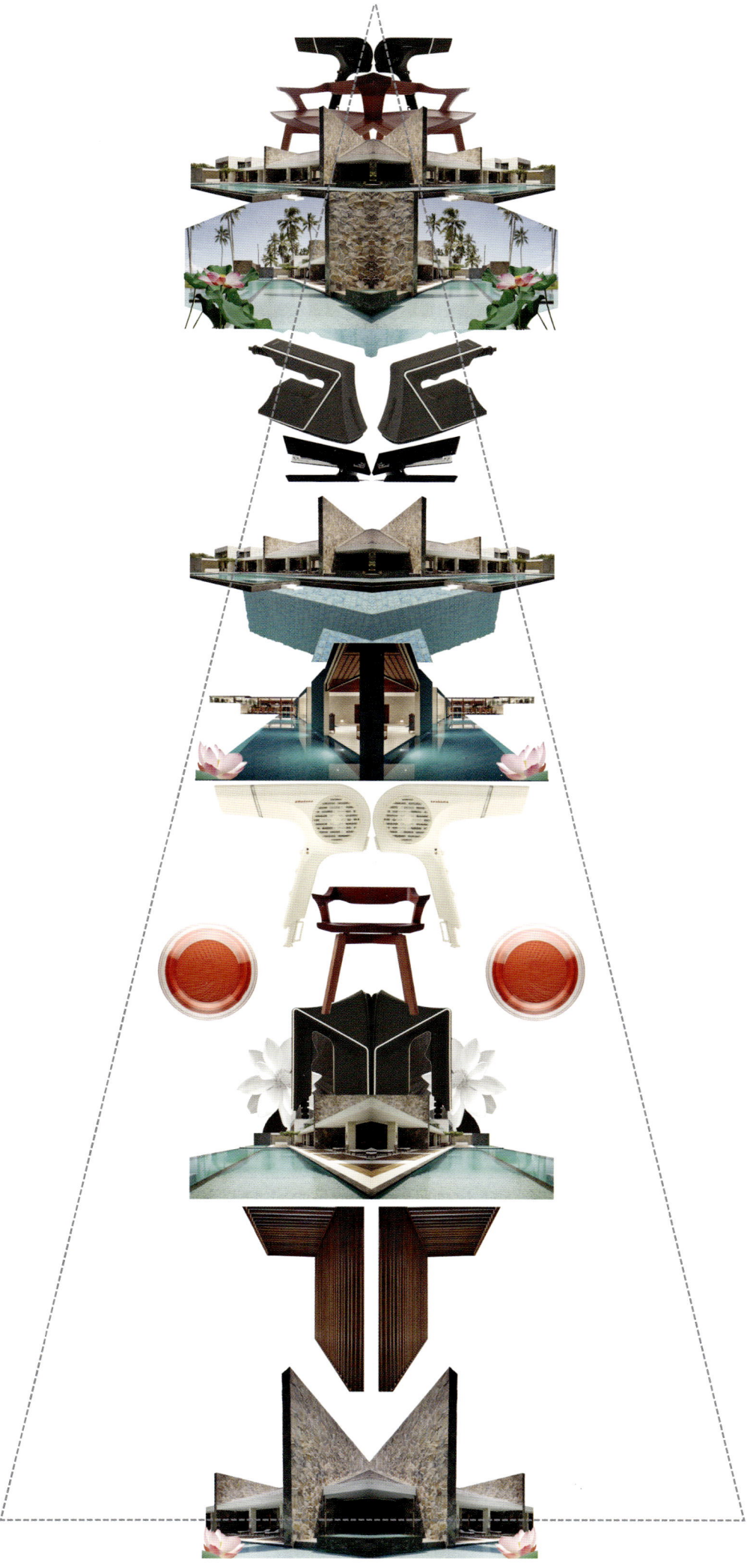

Architecture

Interior   Products

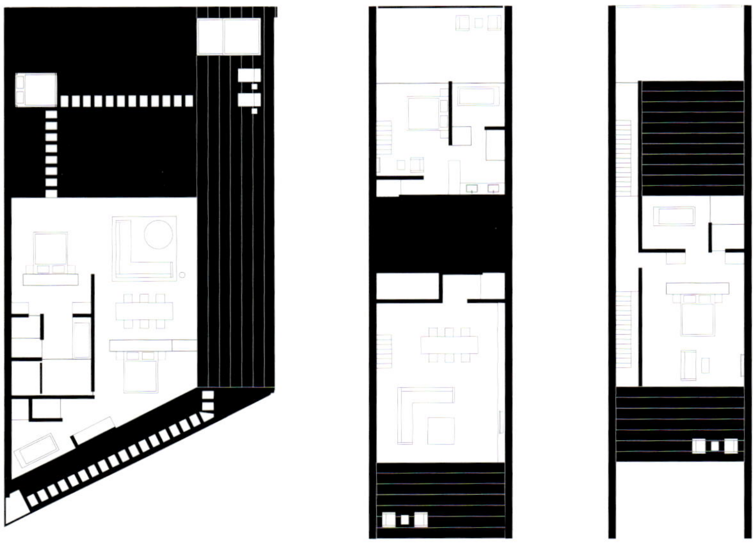

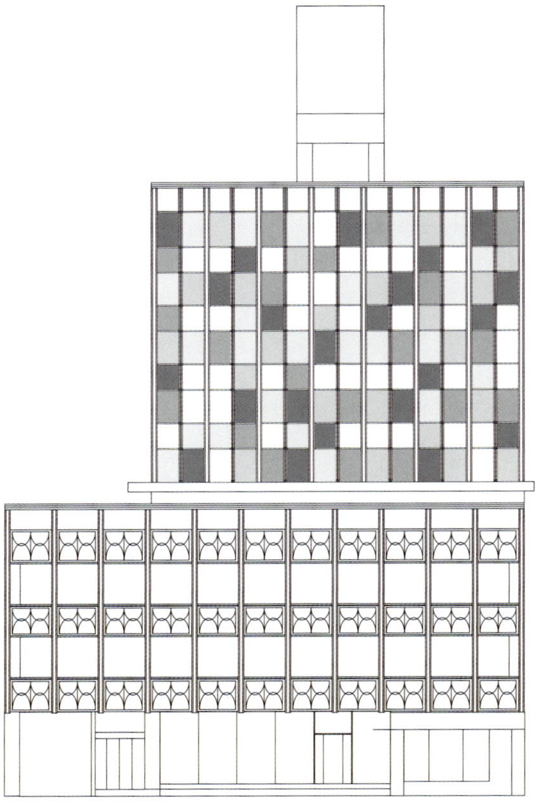

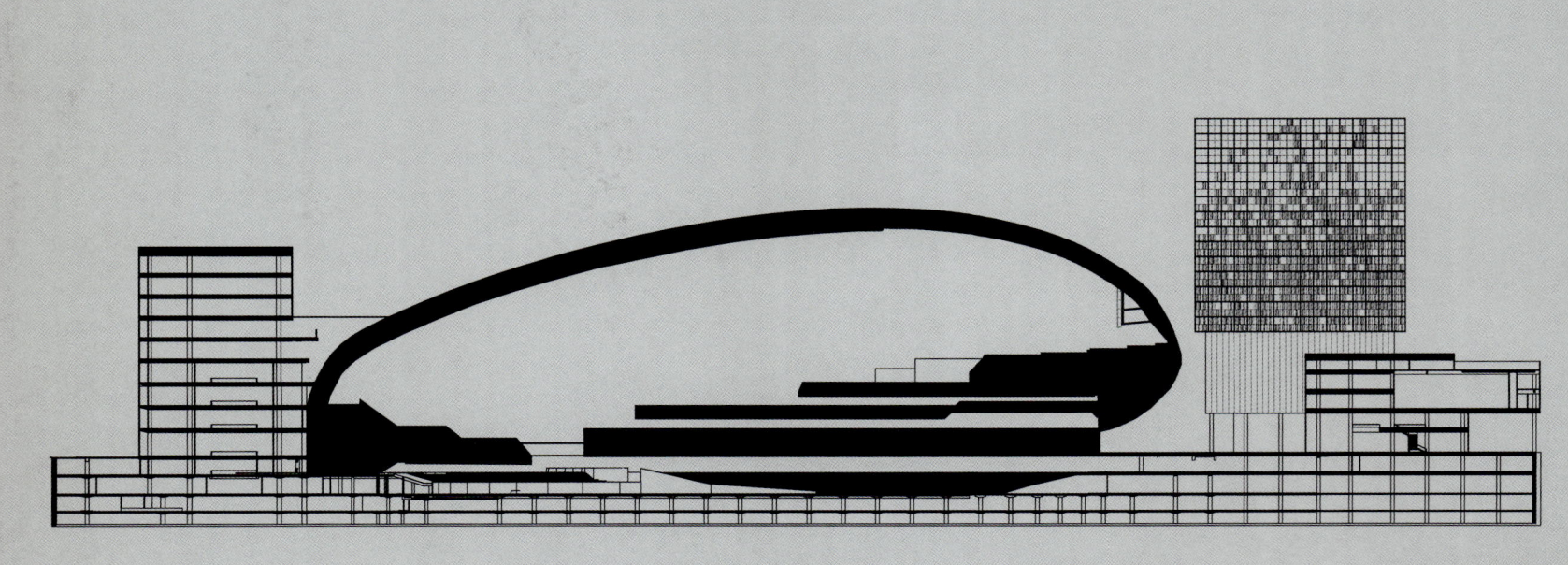

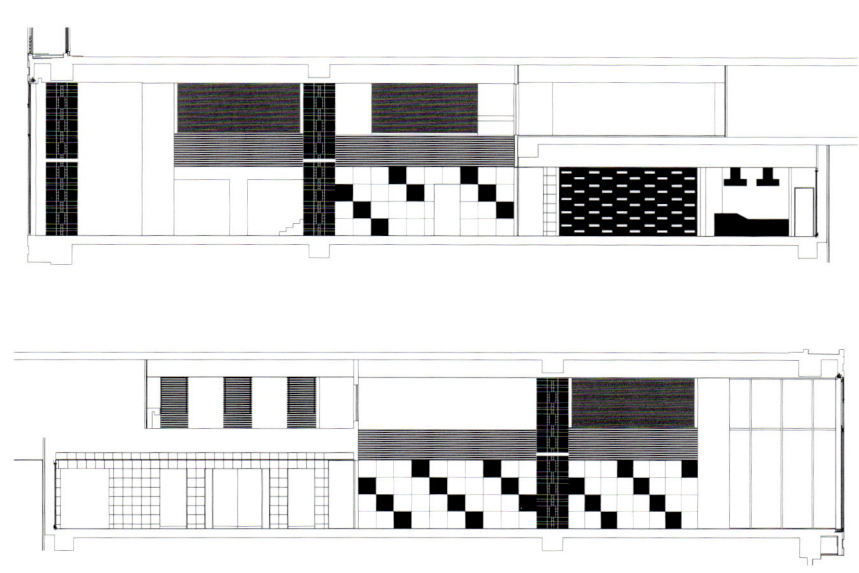

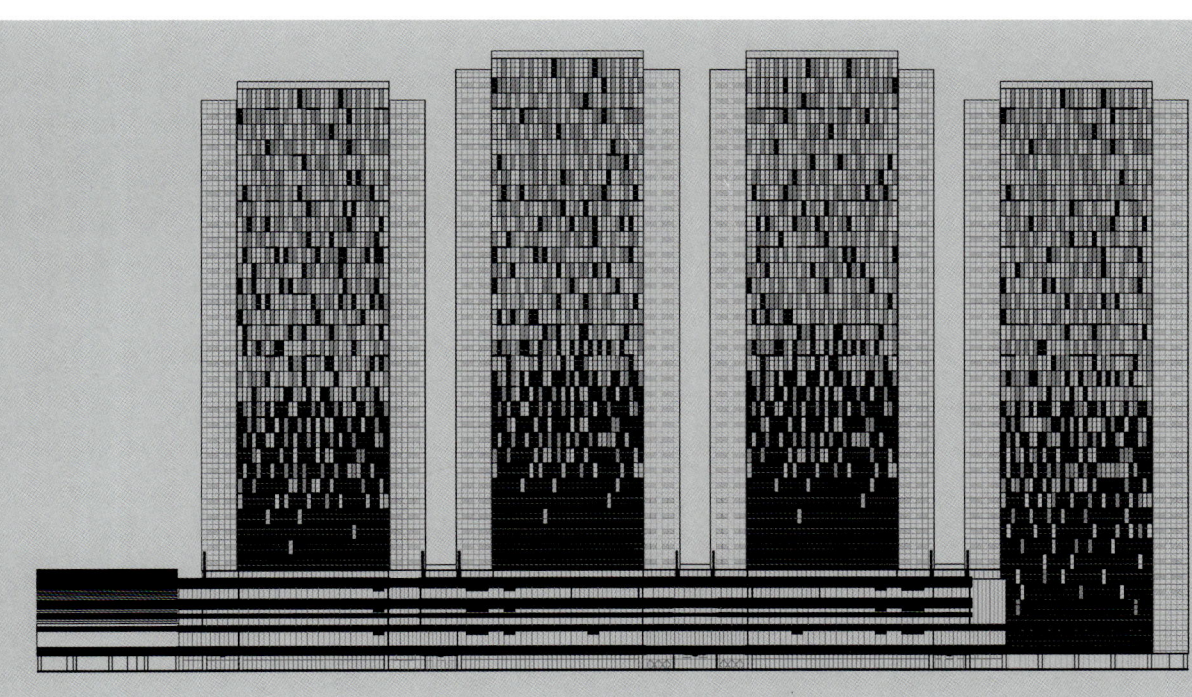

Materiality

In our daily lives, we are surrounded by all types of materials, whether we're conscious of them or not. Intentionallies strives to express the original feel, colour, and form of the materials the firm uses. When designing spaces, Intentionallies believes that the mix and balance of materials is of paramount importance. When creating a space with the warm look of wood, for example, the firm doesn't simply use timber in different applications, but also considers its relationship with other materials, and how a blend will bring out the beauty of the main material. To accomplish this, the special characteristics and appearance of the specific material are taken into account, along with the best type of coating to use to achieve the desired finish. Revealing the essential beauty of a material is, to Intentionallies, materiality.

A Collection of Elegant Design Tools

Following the amadana and Hotel Claska projects, Intentionallies wanted the challenge of designing a range of small, refined products. Craft Design Technology presented itself, and the 40-piece collection of office-related supplies is now considered one of the firm's three most groundbreaking projects. The firm was pleased to have decided, with the client group, to select stationery, as, explains Shuwa Tei, 'We use it ourselves when designing.'

The client group was made up of stationery experts, each of whom had specialized in one or two office products, and had joined forces to set up the new brand. Leading the group was the owner of one of Japan's oldest wholesaler stationery distributors. Intentionallies suggested the products to be included in the collection, and then designed the entire line. Together with the London-based brand-ing agency Winkreative, the firm worked not just on the style of the products, but also on the image of the collection, ensuring the overall presentation of the line reflected its core values.

The collection ranges from pens and scissors to sellotape dispensers, folders and more. Each item was produced using the expertise and technologies the clients had developed for their own products. Intentionallies advised the client group not to market the range only to stationery stores, but also via the 200-plus retailers across Japan that were already stock-ists of Intentionallies' amadana line. Selling the products at lifestyle shops was an integral aspect of the brand's success. Tei elaborates, 'This approach enabled us to present the products to consumers as a complete collec-tion from a new stationery brand, instead of selling them as separate, unconnected items.'

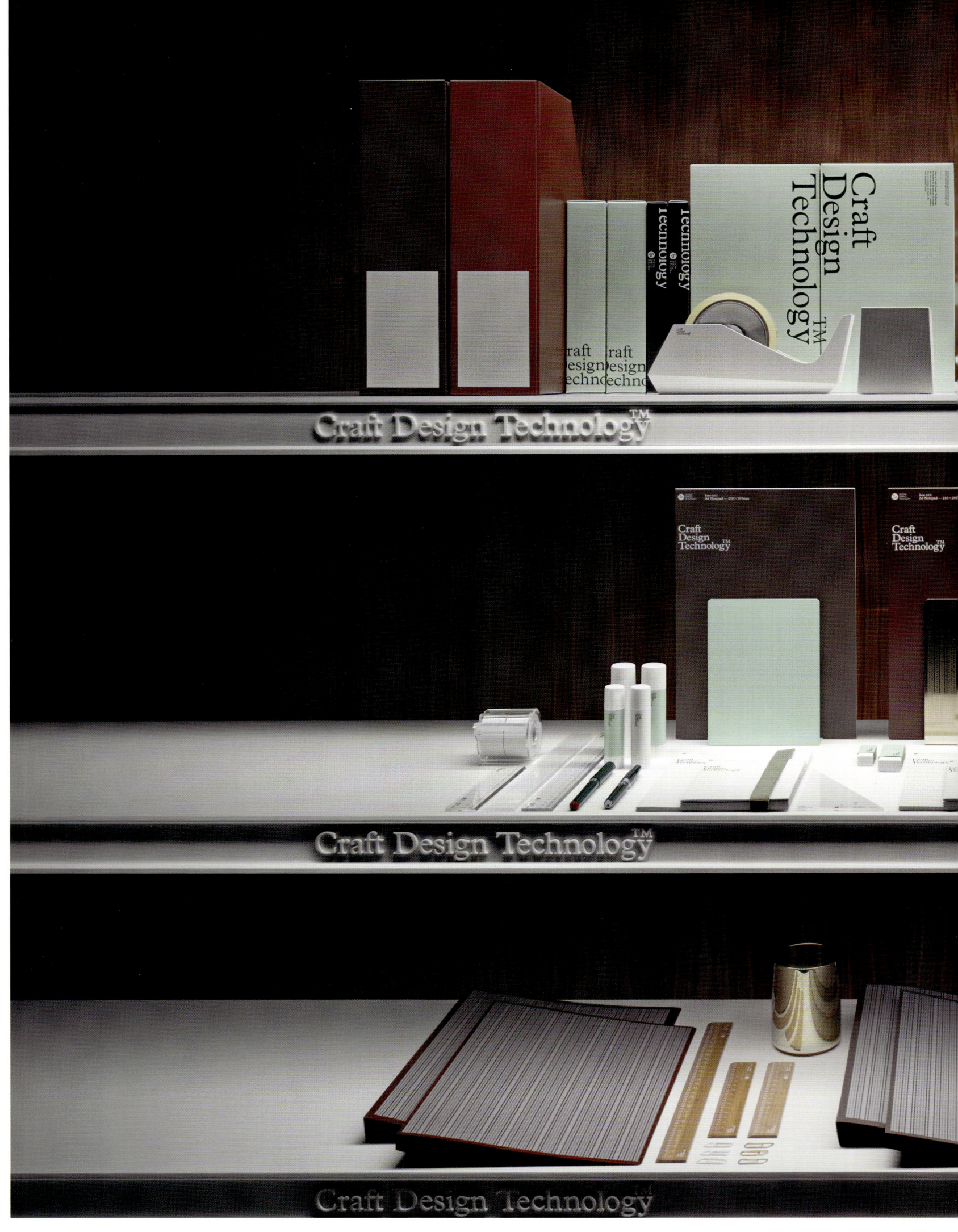

Intentionallies — Materiality

The latest addition to the amadana line is a mobile phone. The design parameters were so tight,
Intentionallies had to evolve its philosophy in order to implement the desired remodelling.

N705i

amadana mobile - SEG display design

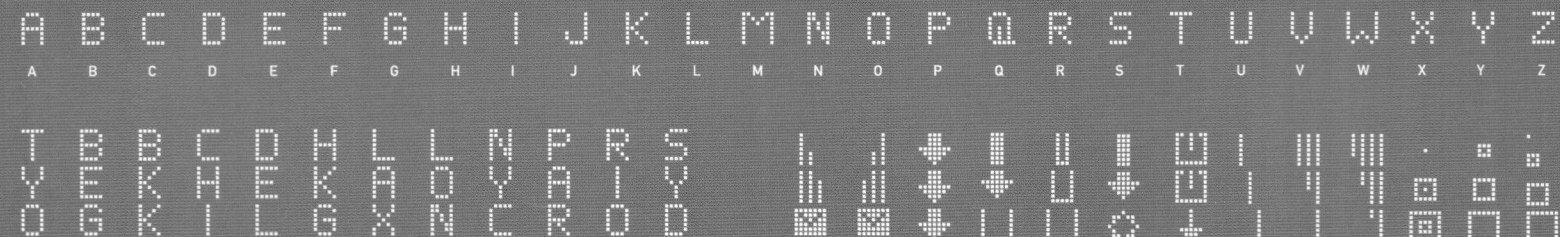

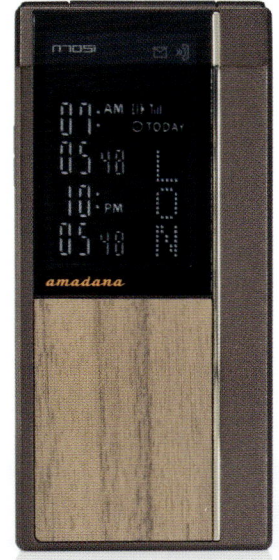

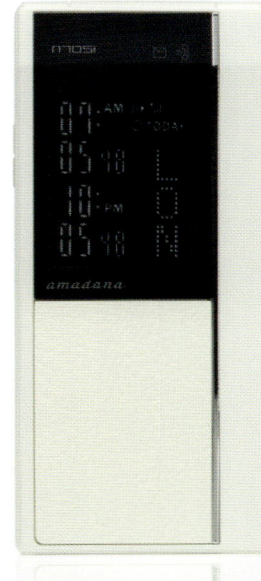

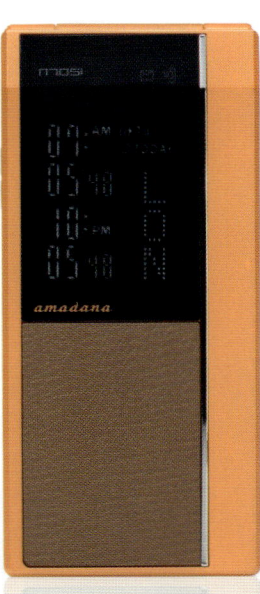

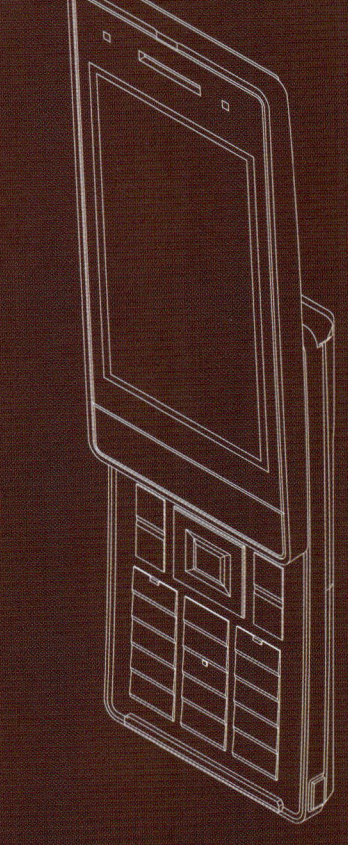

N04-A

amadana signature

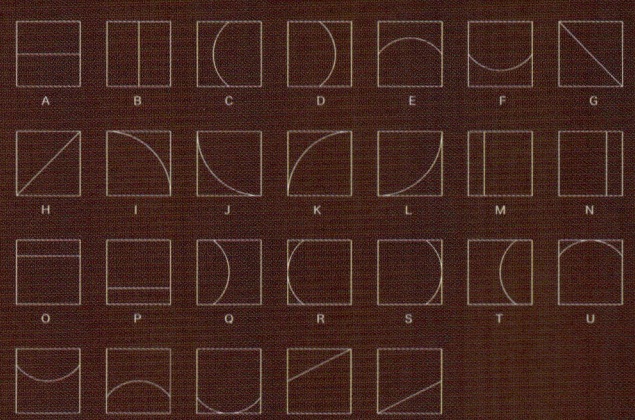

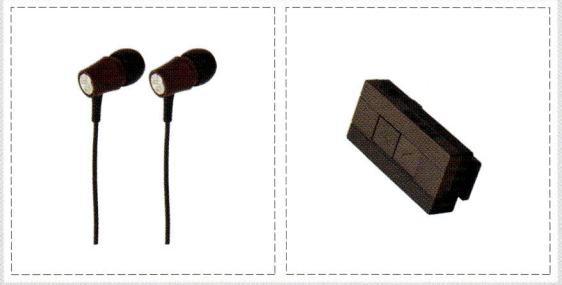

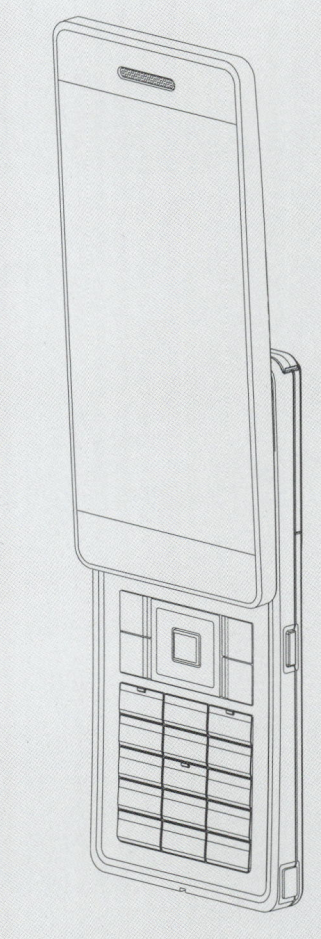

Materiality

Intentionallies

N07-B

Contents design

From Large-Scale Constructions to Mobile Phones

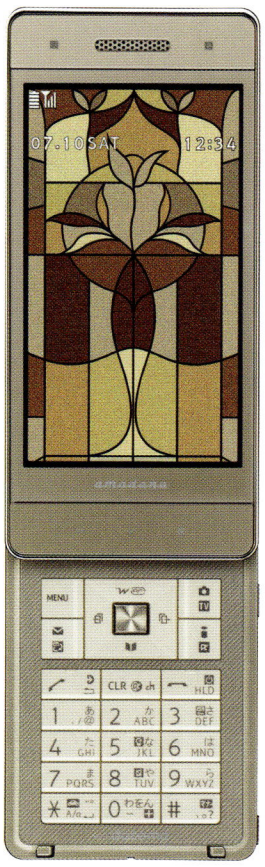 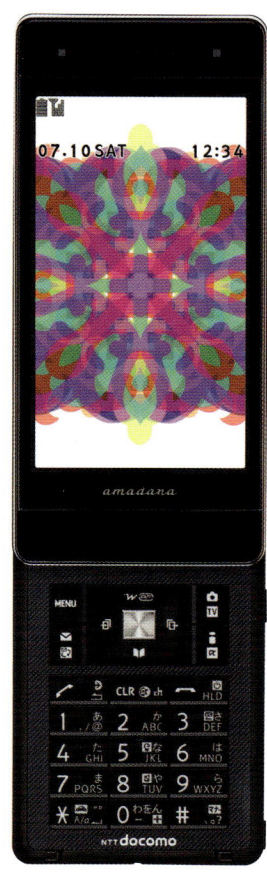  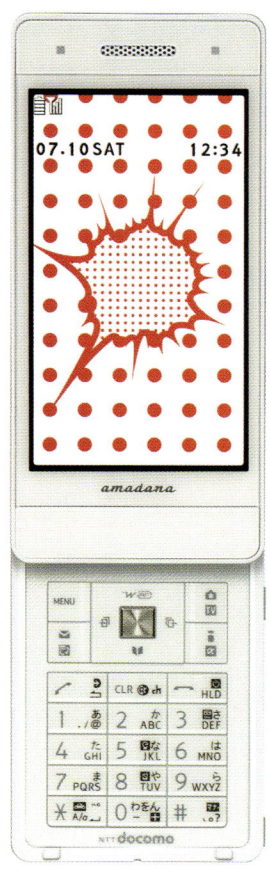

If Intentionallies were asked, 'Why is an architectural design firm designing mobile phones?' the answer would be that it is an appropriate response to the changing nature of public buildings. Until recently, public buildings have been authoritarian spaces, owned by national, prefectural, or municipal entities. However, they have become more open and accessible to the public, and are, sometimes, spaces that a great number of people can share. 'For us,' says Shuwa Tei, 'The design solutions for mobile phones share a fascinating similarity to those that can be found in architecture. This relationship is one that tends to be overlooked due to the differences in scale.'

The design of a mobile phone begins by establishing a viewpoint. The next step is sifting through hundreds or thousands, if not tens of thousands, of parameters in order to crystallize what beauty is, from that perspective. An absolute condition of a successful outcome is finding the single, perfect form from a myriad of possible alternatives. The result is also impacted by the selection of functions considered necessary; the physical size of parts; the limitations presented by the layout of parts, and the price/performance relationship. Working through the process requires the monotonous editing of a huge mass of data and the making of instant judgments while being fully aware of the effect of each choice. Tei states simply, 'All decisions rely on this process.'

Intentionallies | Materiality

The Eco digi Mode is a use-and-recycle digital camera that Intentionallies designed as a core brand product for the photo development chain Palette Plaza. Each camera's LCD panel was a recycled part, taken from a discarded mobile phone. In a nostalgic nod to traditional film development and printing, it was not possible to edit the pictures taken, although the user was given 10 seconds after taking each shot to decide whether or not to erase it.

When Intentionallies was researching the project, the firm realized that a number of mobiles were being discarded because their owners had upgraded to new phones with the latest specifications. This represented an untapped resource as the LCD panels still functioned perfectly. The cameras were to be sold only at Palette Plaza, where the photos would be burned onto a CD. Adding to the eco credentials of the project, once the photos had been removed from the camera's memory, the returned camera could then be resold.

Unfortunately, a practical problem arose because Intentionallies was unable to obtain sufficient numbers of discarded phones, so the project was reclassified as a one-off. 'However,' says Shuwa Tei, 'Eco digi Mode was still a very meaningful attempt to craft an attractive, recycled and recyclable product.'

Integrating a Recycled Mobile Phone Part into a Camera

Using a Design Code
to Shape a Pairs of Glasses

When establishing the design concept for several pairs of glasses for the eyewear specialist JINS, Intentionallies felt the firm's high-quality, affordable glasses required a strong brand identity. Intentionallies carried out extensive research to understand how the glasses were made and concluded that a reference system was needed to ensure frames and materials were combined to best effect. The firm devised a diagram to serve this purpose. Next, Intentionallies looked at how to make glasses a comfortable fit, a vital consideration given the range of individual face shapes and the frequency with which glasses are put on and

taken off. Intentionallies came up with the acronym FRAMES, containing the six elements that the firm believed were fundamental to glasses design, which stands for functional, rational, aesthetic, material, exchangeable, and style. The word became the design code used as the starting point for all JINS products.

Working with the diagram and acronym, Intentionallies designed several signature models using 3D software to shape the glasses. The CAD program gave the team the freedom to sculpt the desired forms by cutting into a 3D volume.

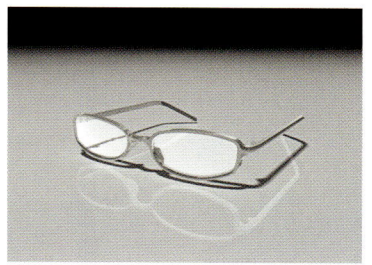
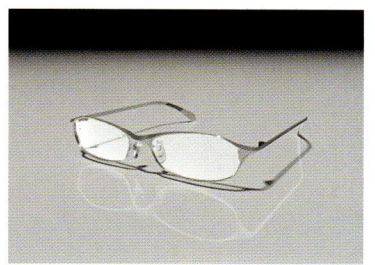

Collaborating with Craftsman

Furniture creates the character of a space, and chairs, in particular, give structure and shape to an interior. 'Sitting on a chair is a custom that has its origins in Western culture,' says Shuwa Tei, 'Traditionally, in Japan, people sat on the floor, but we've long since adapted to using chairs. As a creator, I have always thought it was better to use a chair, however exceptional, and not just revere it as a work of artistry.'

Instead of buying in furniture for each project, Intentionallies designs all its furnishings in collaboration with craftsmen who are invited to express what they think would work in each specific interior. The artisans, who are very skilled in the production of furniture, reinterpret traditional approaches and use modern techniques to create distinctive pieces that are valued by clients. The collaboration process began in 1999 and has evolved into a strong relationship.

Rather than forming an independent line available to the public, the pieces are solely for Intentionallies to use in its own projects. The first furniture to be produced was exhibited as a collection in 2001 at a show called Fusion to Define the Meanings by Architecture and Intentionallies has gone from strength to strength since.

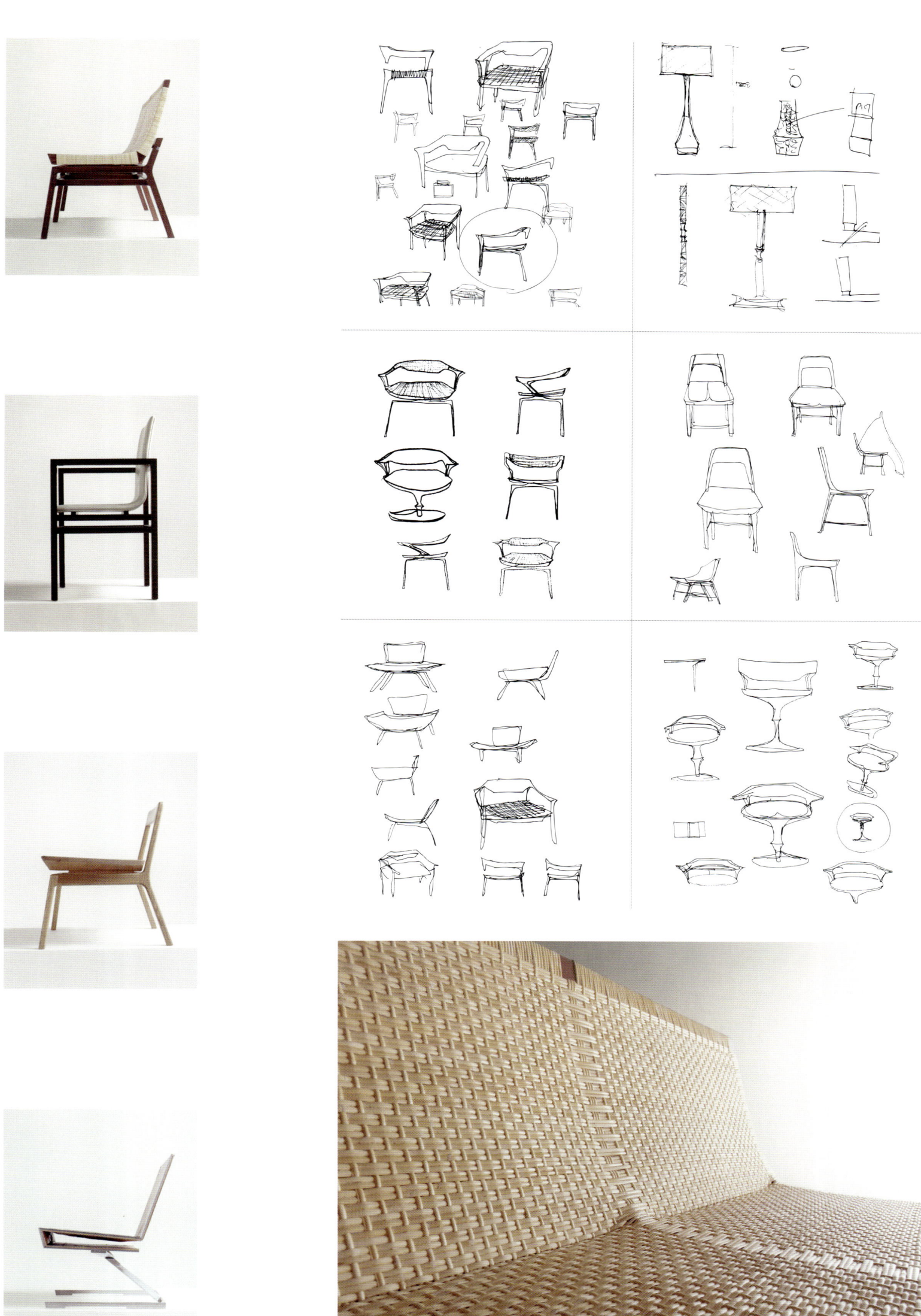

An Elegant Collection
of Home Appliances

In today's dining environment, home appliances are used regularly but the majority are dismissed as nothing more than electric equipment because they are not in harmony with the colour and form of the food served.

Intentionallies responded to the way home appliances are regarded by developing a line called the atehaca collection. The name given to the collection defines it, as *atehaca* is an old Japanese word meaning elegance, and is a derivative of the word for noble. In Japan, plateware complements the food served, and vice versa. Visual appeal is even important in the preparation of bento, the single portion takeout or home-packed lunch box. An inherent part of food presentation is, says Shuwa Tei, 'The beauty of the margin, because it defines the serving as a painting.' This is where Japanese aesthetics come into play. Tei explains, 'We asked ourselves why appliances aren't as attractive, in terms of their shape and hue, as they could be. Shouldn't they possess the same elegance as the furniture in the dining space?' Intentionallies then proceeded to investigate forms reminiscent of dishes; colours that enhanced food, and dining areas that looked dignified even with appliances stored onsite.

Japanese home appliances are renowned for having poorly integrated basic functions, such as switches and displays, resulting in products that are not visually appealing. Faced with the challenge of creating products that didn't have bulky control buttons, Intentionallies took inspiration from pictographs, an intrinsic part of Japan's cultural history. Together with the Tokyo-based graphic design agency Tycoon Graphics, the firm used pictograms to communicate the functions of the appliances clearly and strongly, giving atehaca products a sleek profile.

'We believe that to design is to create meaning, rather than simply recreating variations of a form,' states Tei. One of the principles underpinning the collection takes a stand against a throwaway society. 'If a striking product functions well, its owners will handle it with care, and keep it for a long period,' says Tei. Mass production has led to a culture based on consumerism and, inevitably, waste. 'But,' says Tei, 'Shoppers respond when they're reminded of the value of longevity. The atehaca products provide positive affirmation that what is beautiful can also be permanent.' Intentionallies plans to take the philosophy one step further by using recyclable and biodegradable materials for atehaca products in the future.

The essence of Japan's food culture is the food, plateware and bento boxes that are used everyday. The atehaca collection offers a welcome extension to the traditional elements, because the appliances complement the food, the furniture required to house them and the dining room setting itself. Says Tei, 'We are committed to creating products that not only have attractive exteriors, but also function beautifully, creating elegant, dignified items.'

Materiality

Intentionallies

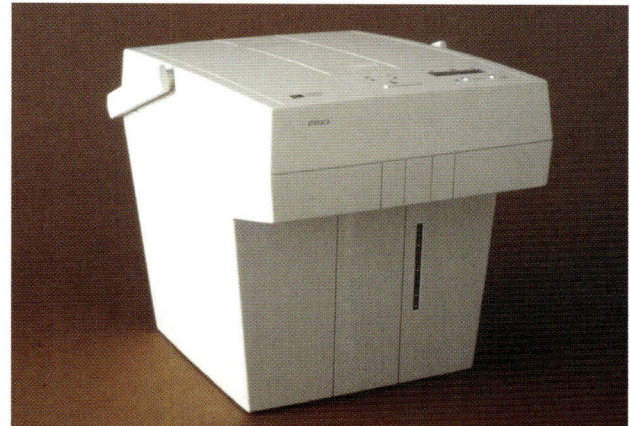

Materiality

Intentionallies

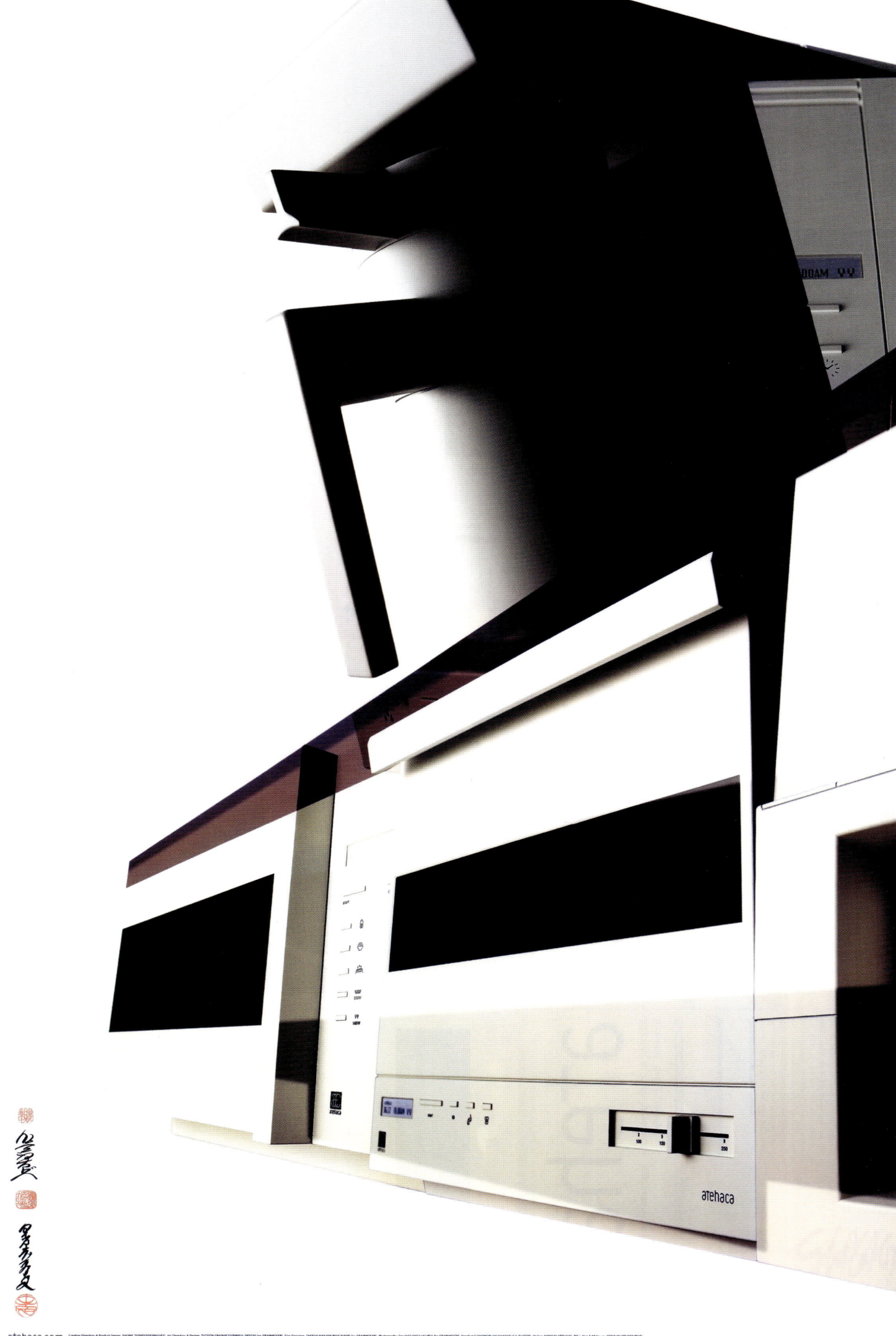

A Laptop Dressed in Leather

A laptop is an important tool and is one that has evolved rapidly over the last few decades. You only have to think back to your first laptop to see how swiftly the advances have been made. Each newly released model is faster, lighter and equipped with the latest technologies and the highest specifications, capable of being used for ever-more complex tasks. However, in the early 2000s, the upgrades didn't extend as far as the appearance of a laptop; beauty and texture were not a main consideration.

With this in mind, Toshiba approached Realfleet, the firm that Shuwa Tei founded in 2002 with Masaki Tabei and Hiroshi Kumamoto (former Toshiba employees) to redesign electronics. Toshiba asked Realfleet to design a co-branded laptop that was to be a limited edition, with a production run of just 500. Shuwa Tei and his team set out to create a laptop that was attractive,

which users would become attached to.

The result was dynabook, a laptop whose lid popped open to reveal a keyboard in three tones, with rows of either chocolate brown, off-white or caramel keys. The colours complement a palm rest in tan leather, a material choice that adds an ironic touch, as it juxtaposes its traditional feel with the digital laptop it wraps. Stamped in a corner of the luxurious-looking leather is the serial number of each laptop, running from 001 to 500, emphasizing the exclusivity of the product. The laptop was completed with a mouse and a custom-designed leather case, also in tan. The leather was fluorinated, to protect it from marks or stains. The appeal of the laptops was apparent in sales figures; distributed via apparel and home furnishings boutiques, they all sold within three weeks.

Intentionallies Materiality

17LX10

ON TIMER   ON ——— BLUE
            STANDBY —— RED

右—音声—左 映像
ビデオ入力2
▶S映像
ヘッドホン
右—音声—左 音声出力

One Set of Moulds for Two TVs, One Exclusive and One for the Consumer Market

Televisions are found in most homes. Towards the end of the 20th century, the presence of a television could even be taken as an indicator of a certain standard of living. Some people can't be in a room with a TV without switching it on and when a television is on, it's almost impossible not to watch it. The face-to-face nature of television viewing was what Shuwa Tei and his team focused on during the design of a television commissioned by Toshiba, who chose Face, post-production, as the name of the TV. The television was crafted as part of Realfleet, the firm that Shuwa Tei founded in 2002 together with two former Toshiba employees to redesign electronics.

The television has an LCD screen – the latest technology when Face was first released – giving it a slender profile. The monitor is bordered by a lacquer frame that is polished to a piano finish, equating to nine or 10 applications. The display is mounted on a stand of brushed stainless steel, a finish more usually used for furniture than televisions. Incorporated into the design is a handle wrapped in tan leather, giving a comfortable grip when lifting the TV. The back and side views of the TV were taken into account during the design process, resulting in a product that is attractive from all angles.

Borrowing a business model from the fashion world, Realfleet produced two versions of the TV from the same moulds. In addition to the exclusive 'couture' model described above, Realfleet produced a 'prêt-à-porter' version for the more mainstream consumer market, with different finishes and materials, for example, a plastic, not stainless steel stand. With the launch of Face, Tei intended that the classification of certain televisions would be transferred from home appliances to living room furniture, elevated by the distinctive details of his products.

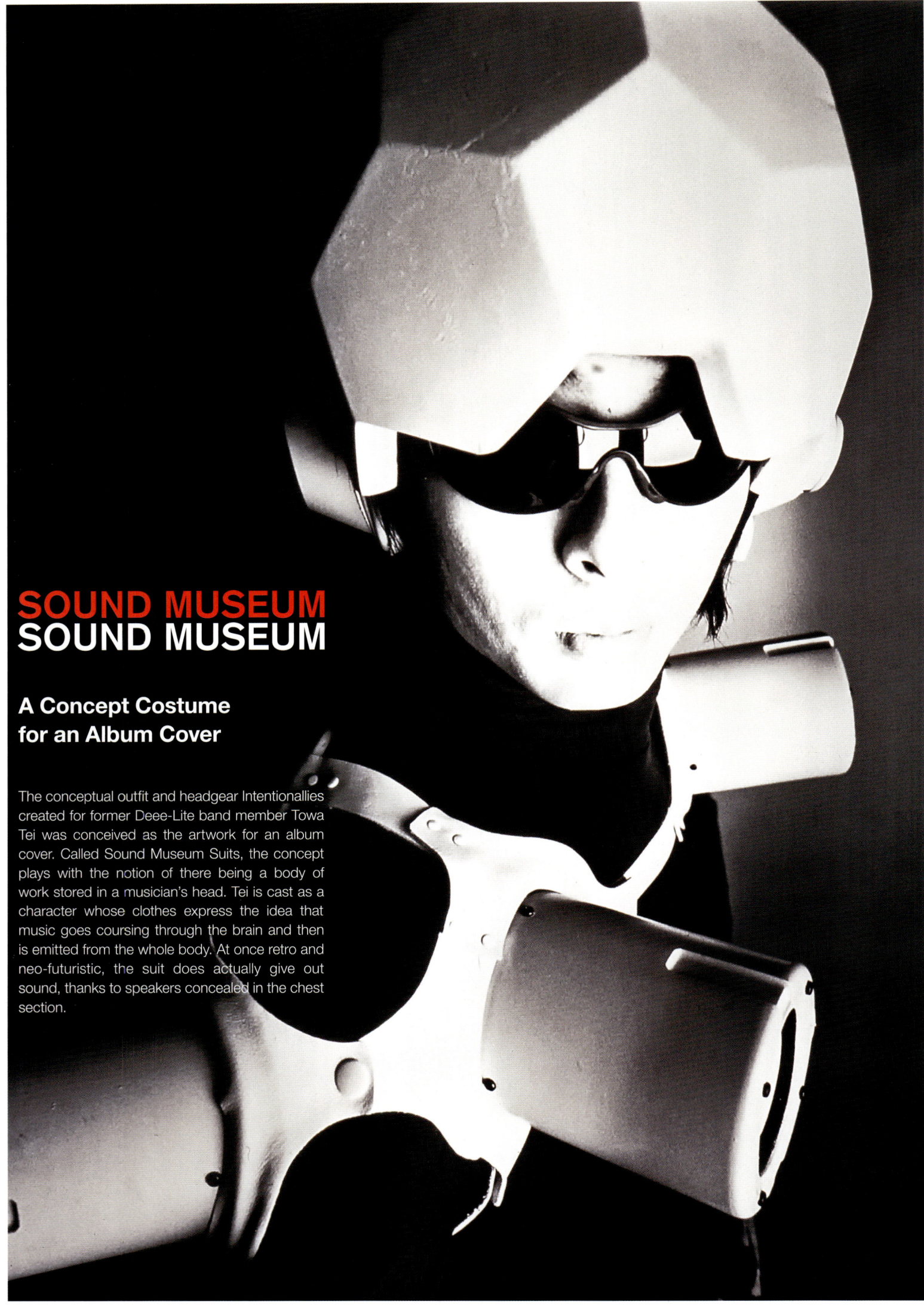

Materiality

Intentionallies

SOUND MUSEUM
SOUND MUSEUM

A Concept Costume
for an Album Cover

The conceptual outfit and headgear Intentionallies created for former Deee-Lite band member Towa Tei was conceived as the artwork for an album cover. Called Sound Museum Suits, the concept plays with the notion of there being a body of work stored in a musician's head. Tei is cast as a character whose clothes express the idea that music goes coursing through the brain and then is emitted from the whole body. At once retro and neo-futuristic, the suit does actually give out sound, thanks to speakers concealed in the chest section.

A Compact Collection of Fittings for Hotel Guest Rooms

A collection of hotel room fittings, designed by Realfleet, share an elegant, understated design code, making them suitable for use in many different styles of hotel interiors. Comprising a kettle, coffee maker, telephone, hairdryer, alarm clock, LCD television and remote control, the line of products is called barouche after a 19th century carriage. The nostalgic nod to horse-drawn travel is actually indicative of how Shuwa Tei intends the fittings to be used. If lots of hotels use the barouche line, as is planned, then each time a guest stays in one of those rooms they will be surrounded by the same fittings. This has the effect of making the collection as familiar as if that guest had brought the items along with them, as a traveller would have done in times past, when a large trunk would have been packed with (less technical but nonetheless everyday) necessities. In this way, Realfleet has provided hotel guests with tools for travel.

Aside from one or two obvious items, the pared down profile of the pieces in the collection could result in the function of each being somewhat ambiguous. To counter this, Realfleet engraved, rather than printed, the instructions for use onto the products, imbuing each with an exclusive feel. In standard hotel rooms, each product is usually from a different brand, creating a mismatch look that is anything but universal. The barouche line, however, is made principally from white ABS plastic, giving the collection a shared aesthetic, which is a welcome contrast to the alternatives.

Intentionallies ▬ *Materiality*

coffee maker BR-01

A compact-size coffee maker with quality features.
This double-walled mug makes fresh coffee to stay warm for several hours.
You will enjoy the sip of coffee just as you desire to get, and carry it on the go.

Size: W 135 x D 210 x H 270 mm
rating: 100V(50-60Hz), rated power consumption: 500W, capacity: 270cc
safety functions: thermo fuse

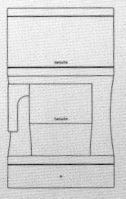

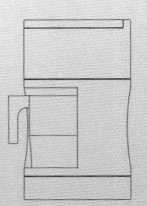

kettle BR-02

An electronic kettle has long been appreciated in European countries.
The beauty of its function comes from its ability to boil water in very short time.
With handiness and lightness, it sets a standard for Tea time Conoisseurs.

Size: W 135 x D 210 x H 270 mm
rating: 100V(50-60Hz), rated power consumption: 1200W, capacity: 1.2L
safety functions: thermo fuse, thermo stat

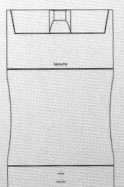  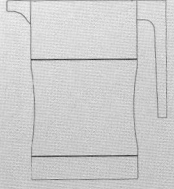

Intentionallies ▌ *Materiality*

alarm clock   BR-03

An alarm clock perfectly brings you the elegant awaking.
It not only has sleek, minimal appearance and universal
navigation but also plays original mellow sound for your awakening.

Size: W 175 × H 44 × D 14 mm
other functions: current time display, alarm, global time display,
thermometer, snooze, backlighted LCD

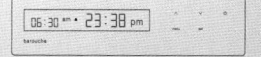
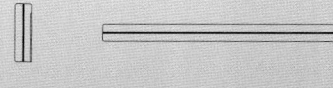

Promotional Products for a Champagne House

When champagne producer Krug asked Intentionallies to design a series of promotional products suitable for a ritual or ceremony, the design practice began by looking at Krug's philosophy. Shuwa Tei explains, 'Our interpretation was that Krug had high aspirations and cared enormously about craftsmanship.' The team at Intentionallies observed that the two firms had much in common, with Krug, like Intentionallies, applying cutting edge technologies to its work, and focusing intently on the finest of details to get the aesthetics just right.

Intentionallies visualized the term 'ritual' as the opening of a bottle of champagne, and the sense of occasion that the popping of a cork carries. The design firm noted that there is no universal way of handling the cork once the champagne has been opened, and, in addition, felt that something was needed to mark the symbolic moment. The first product the firm produced was an acrylic cork holder. It stands out as a veritable art object on the table when a cork is placed into it. Intentionallies also designed an ice bucket wrapped in white leather. The firm collaborated with Japanese furniture makers to devise a way of applying the fine leather, more usually used in upholstery, onto the solid aluminium pieces. In addition to the champagne cooler, a tray, lined in white leather, and acrylic display units, both countertop and standalone, were designed by Intentionallies and added to the collection.

The Design Philosophy
Behind amadana

It is a well-known fact that, following World War II, Japan experienced a period of spectacular economic growth and became a major power with one of the largest economies in the world. Its success was largely due to the country making the most of its technical capabilities, and was partly supported by the manufacturing of home appliances.

In the mid-1990s, however, the period of tremendous prosperity ended as Japan's economy plummeted into a recession. But positive growth in the early 21st century signalled the beginnings of a recovery. In 2003, Shuwa Tei decided it was time to respond to a growing demand in the home appliances market and, in a nod to history, Realfleet, the firm that Tei had founded in 2002 with two former Toshiba employees, began producing electro-domestic appliances. The Realfleet collection has a conscious, Japanese aesthetic and is crafted to a high technical standard.

In what is now Tokyo's Nihonbashi district, there was, during the Edo era (from 1600 to the 1860s) a neighbourhood called Amadana that boasted a considerable number of Japanese lacquer craftsmen and wholesale lacquer merchants. Today, lacquerware is considered one of the symbols of the Japanese aesthetic consciousness as it represents both Japanese technology and beauty. (Because of this, Japanese lacquerware is even called 'Japan' overseas.) As Realfleet selected these qualities as the defining characteristics for its line of home appliances, it made sense for the collection to be called amadana.

There are two criteria that determine the selection of appliances for the amadana line. Firstly, the context that Tokyo is set in, because traditional lifestyles are being replaced with lifestyles governed by convenience and consumerism. Shuwa Tei explains that 'amadana is an expression of our response to appliance usage in Tokyo, and the collection maintains a delicate balance between the complex aspects of

city life'. The second relates to the fact that a 24-hour culture is no longer restricted to capital cities like Tokyo. Extended working hours, brought on by non-traditional shifts and the need for interaction on an international scale, have reached unprecedented levels. The knock-on-effects have permeated our professional, social and domestic lives. Answering the demand for equipment that brings everyday convenience is the amadana line.

'The products in the collection,' says Tei, 'Are objects of outstanding workmanship that project a warmth in appearance and represent forward-thinking minimalism.' He continues, 'We believe that home appliances should be the first elements that are selected when clients are defining the style of their residential space.' The home appliance line is just the beginning. The firm has plans to continue developing the range, by adding products that help consumers 'establish the lifestyle that best represents them, whether through portable devices or communication equipment,' explains Tei.

amadana

Intentionallies   Materiality

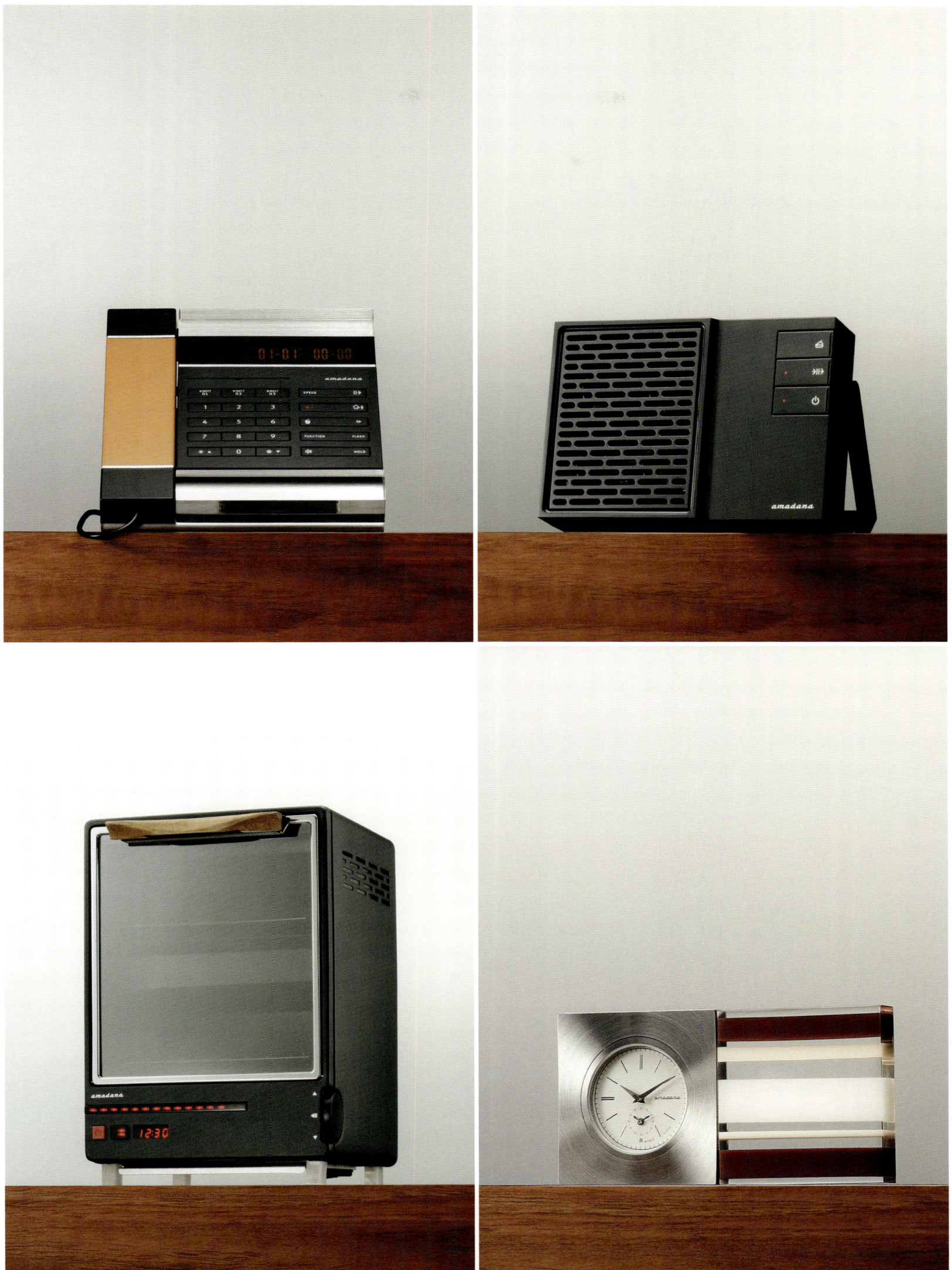

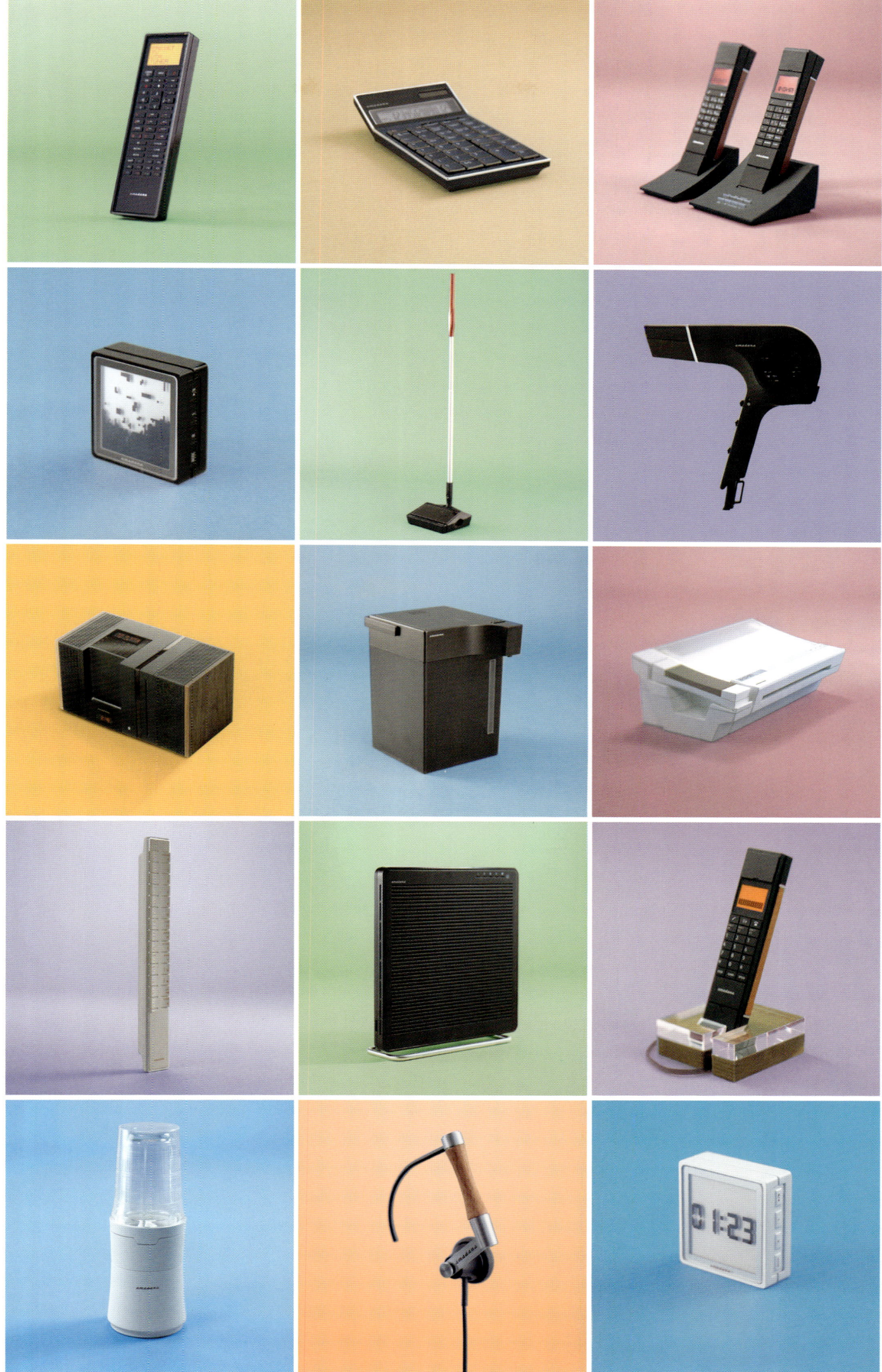

Intentionallies   Materiality

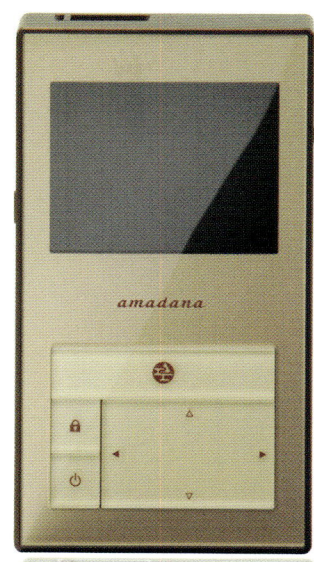

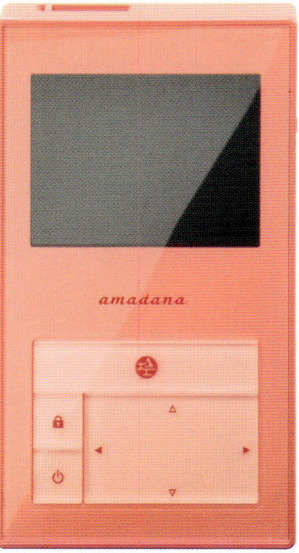

Dealing with Gravity

Craftsmanship through architecture is Intentionallies' creed. The definition of three-dimensional is becoming ever wider and in the future, it may change further still. Shuwa Tei comments, 'To me, three-dimensional means spatialization, which starts with architecture and proceeds on through everything else.' He continues, 'When I first started studying architecture, I felt that in the main, what I was studying referred to structures. We eventually designed a building, but I strongly felt that I had to explore and experiment more first.' investigating the visual and emotional impact of inflatable structures, Intentionallies used balloons to play with gravity, making, as ever, an honest connection between different elements.

Fabric for a Fashion Show

For a catwalk show and exhibition staged by fashion magazine Cutie in Harajuku, Intention-allies used non-flammable fabric – draped over furniture and suspended from the ceiling – to create an atmospheric backdrop.

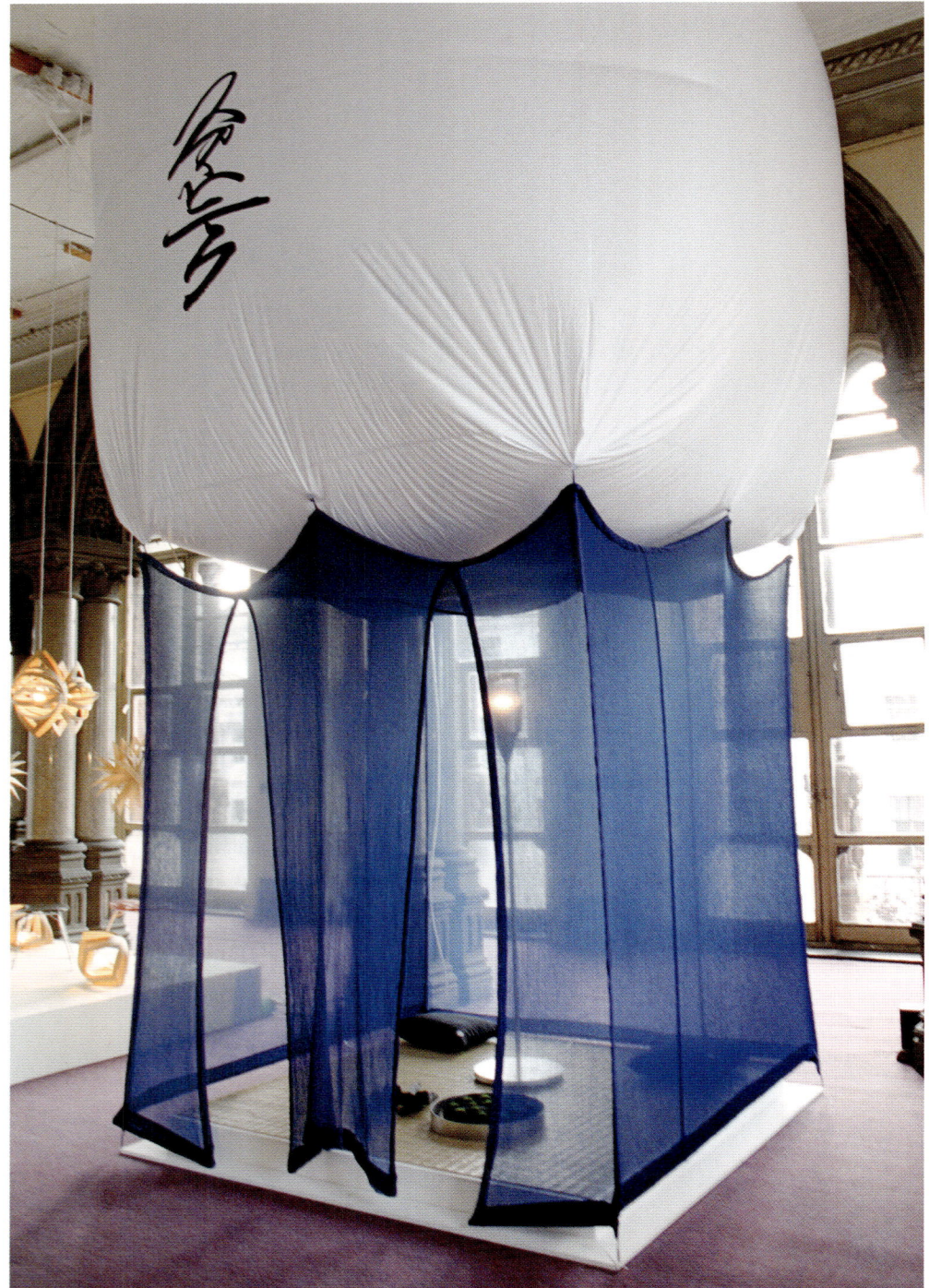

A Space for Meditation

For an installation at Designersblock, Intentionallies collaborated with several Japanese artisans to craft a space for meditation. The project was one of the firm's first overseas assignments and so Intentionallies set out to capture the essence of meditation in a Japanese context.

Bamboo matting laid out on the floor defined the meditation area. As Japanese ceilings are usually lower than those in Western buildings, Intentionallies installed a single, massive, custom-made balloon over the mat. This effectively established a new, lower ceiling directly above the matting. To further distinguish the meditation space from the large room it was located in, Intentionallies hung a fine net around the perimeter of the balloon and anchored it to the mat below. The inflated balloon naturally pulled the netting and mat upward, creating the illusion that the meditation space was almost floating. Made of hemp and dyed indigo blue, the netting was impregnated with the uplifting scent of cypress. When netting of this sort is used indoors in Japan, for example in a bedroom, the netting is said to create a sacred space. With such associations, the meditation space needed to be purified. This was done, again according to tradition, by placing an arrangement of chukka on the floor – chukka being a culturally significant variety of charcoal, considered to purify air; it has an almost flower-like form. The solidity of the charcoal provided a sharp contrast to the fragile netting structure.

For the furnishings, skilled craftspeople made thread from bincho, another kind of charcoal. The strands were woven into fabric, used for the floor cushions. Meanwhile, Edo, a specialized technique for cutting glass that results in light having a very particular flare, was used to make the standing lamp. Before being placed in the meditation space, it was wrapped in a black bamboo shade. Intentionallies subtly underscored the temporal nature of the space, and of meditation itself, with the slogan devised for the exhibit, 'Treasure every encounter'.

Creating a Heavy-looking Structure From Balloons

The stage set that Intentionallies designed for Japanese musician Cornelius played with contrasts to create a convincing illusion. For Cornelius's world tour, Fantasmatic, which opened in Nihon Budokan, Intentionallies crafted a centrepiece that was, in effect, a three-dimensional trompe l'oeil. Two massive grids, which looked as though they'd been shaped from a very sturdy material, were actually made from balloons. Intentionallies even designed the installations to create a false sense of perspective, making the stage seem even bigger than it was in the enormous concert venue.

Transforming Two-dimensional Graphics into Three-dimensional Furniture

Music by Contemporary Production was a large-scale exhibit showcasing the work of a graphic designer. Most of the items on display were CD album covers, either the original size or blown up into posters. This presented Intentionallies with a challenge as the firm's expertise is in three-dimensional rather than two-dimensional forms. The firm's solution was to integrate the images into the fixtures and furniture in the exhibition space.

Intentionallies built a long, wide display table, topped in protective glass, which ran the length of the space. Displayed under the glass, like gems in a jewellery shop, were CD album covers. The table was low enough to double as a bench, offering visitors a place to sit. Elsewhere in the space, artwork mounted on large panels was suspended from circular, street lamp-like fittings. Here too, seating was provided. Benches encircling the stand of each lamp encouraged visitors to sit under the graphic panels. The exhibit was destined to go on tour, so showcasing the artwork on furniture and incorporated into fittings ensured the set up at each new location was quick. By creating an informal environment to view the collection, Intentionallies made the presentation accessible, and enabled visitors to react with each other and the work around them.

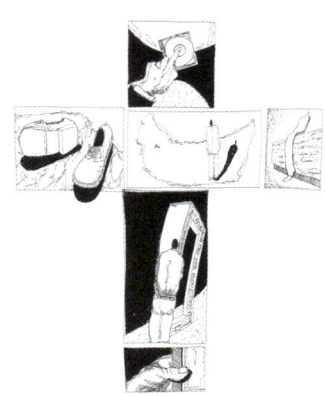
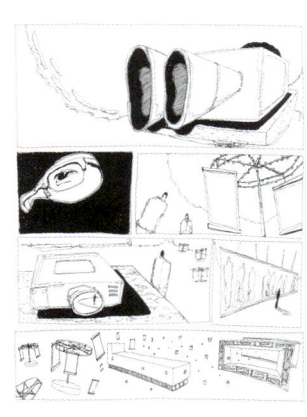

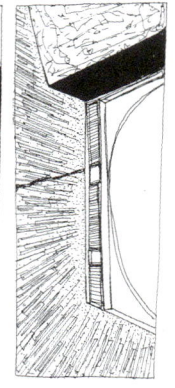

At Home in Tokyo

'I've learnt a great deal about Tokyo just by living in the city,' says Shuwa Tei. 'That is why I felt compelled to found Intentionallies here in Tokyo.' He continues, 'It's vital not to be separated from the city. Living in Tokyo has led me to believe that it is important to be able to constantly define our relationships with society. We need to equip ourselves with the capacity to make definitive judgments about the urban landscape. At Intentionallies we focus on what the word "home" means to us, what it means in architecture, and we strive to create the spaces that we've been dreaming of.'

A Residence With a Furniture-like Extension

An elderly couple wanting to make the most of their retirement commissioned Intentionallies to build a house on a residential block in Takarazuka, near Kobe. The brief requested accommodation that was well ventilated, light-filled and with as few interior partitions as possible. The clients also required space for spare beds for their grown-up son and daughter who visited several times a year. The only condition the clients stipulated was that Intentionallies had to meet a limited budget, which could not exceed ¥25 million, including the design fee.

In order to fulfil these conditions, Intentionallies ran the project as a pilot scheme and developed a blueprint for a house for the elderly. Rather than creating a bespoke design, or haute couture project, the clients were presented with a more universal, or prêt-a-porter, programme, which could then be applied to later projects. To this end, Intentionallies investigated the principal criteria necessary for a living space for older people. The list of requirements the firm complied included wheelchair-friendly entryways, and corridors and doors wide enough to allow a standard wheelchair to pass though. In addition, companionship was of the utmost importance: when an elderly couple who live together are busy doing different tasks, if they were in different areas of one large room, as opposed to being in separate rooms, they would still be able to look across and see each other and even carry on a conversation while occupied with their specific chores. To fulfil this need, large, open rooms were deemed desirable.

Intentionallies designed a cube-shaped, two-storey house. The firm worked hard to keep the house as standard as possible, while meeting the clients' basic needs, to keep costs to a minimum. The design was simple, with the narrow windows on the front of the building mirroring the slatted construction to the rear of the house. The solution Intentionallies came up with that enabled the couple to have open rooms, and also private spaces for when their grown up children came to visit, was simple but effective. As requested, there were no internal walls, but the firm created the possibility for temporary, separate spaces by installing sliding screens. When the screens were pushed back, the rooms resembled big, studio-like spaces where the clients could, as they wished, see and hear each other. Intentionallies then defined each zone within the space with furniture.

The clients had requested the firm make the most of the available sunlight. Intentionallies installed an extension at the rear of the building, with a veranda on the ground floor and a terrace on the first floor. As the sun can be very strong in the area where the house is located, Intentionallies employed slats to function as a louvre system. The structure also offered the owners some privacy from the neighbouring houses. To stay within the budget, Intentionallies installed ready-made aluminium sash windows in the building. These were used throughout the house, except in the pair of windows opening out from the first floor onto the terrace. Aluminium was a functional choice as it offered good insulation – an important consideration as the Kobe area is subject to winter snowfalls. Aluminium frames also proved to be very cost effective and the mechanism was not too technically difficult for the clients to use comfortably. However, the look of the metal was somewhat plain and lacked any feeling of material richness, which the clients had also asked for. To compensate for the

clinical-ooking aluminium, Intentionallies used wood for the sash windows in the living room. The firm also built the veranda and terrace completely out of wood, imbuing the rear of the building with a warmer feel. The wooden structure was also considered as being a piece of furniture. Since talented craftsmen are needed to shape a sound wooden structure, building the veranda and terrace was, in certain respects, similar to shaping a piece of furniture.

Inside the house, Intentionallies opted for wood flooring. The firm chose solid pine, which was treated with an oil finish. The interior walls were given a finely textured finish, obtained using a mixture that included sand grains. The walls themselves contributed to the purity of the air inside the house, as the blend of materials used for plastering was specially selected to maintain the humidity level of the interior. The ceilings were crafted from tannin-finished basswood ply. Selecting a range of different textures of wood was a deliberate choice. Each was carefully chosen for its ageing properties, as over time, the different woods would mature gracefully, adding an extra patina of warmth to the house. In addition, the characteristics of the types of wood chosen complemented the clients' existing furniture and fittings.

As the budget was so limited, the range of materials, structures and finishes open to Intentionallies was very restricted. However, the simple, unfussy house met the specific needs of its occupants, who were delighted to move in even before the wood began to mellow and shrubs and trees started to grow in the garden, transforming the basic cube into a very appealing home.

A Restaurant That Is as Carefully Crafted as the Sushi It Serves

Intentionallies converted the ground and first floors of a house in Tokyo's Nishiazabu district into a sushi and sashimi restaurant. Tucked down an alley, the small restaurant is hard to find, giving it the feel of a private club. In Japan, a sushi chef is considered a master craftsman, so the client requested a finely crafted space to reflect the dishes being served.

Intentionallies began with the tiled steps leading up to the entrance. The discerning diner will notice that the deep green ceramic tiles are similar to *oribe*, a pottery technique used to craft fine dishware. The floor tiles were, in fact, made using the oribe method, neatly reflecting the new function of the building. Inside, in a subtle nod to the building's former use as a residence, guests are required to remove their shoes, a ritual rarely observed in Tokyo. Almost as if to reward diners for their efforts, Intentionallies has laid wood flooring throughout the restaurant that has a particularly pleasant feel underfoot. The wood selected, pau-lownia, is not a commonly seen flooring material as it's more usually used to make boxes to store kimonos in. Intentionallies brought in artisans to carve a wave-like pattern called *naguri* into the surface of the soft wood. The effect is so delicate the wood almost looks sculpted.

The tabletop in the main dining space is made from a single piece of cedar. Measuring almost 6 m long, it was carried into position by no fewer than 10 people. Elsewhere, because the ceilings in the restaurant are quite low (typical of a residential building), guests are seated on the floor. Each low table in this area is positioned over a recess in the floor, allowing diners to sit comfortably on floor seats with their feet in the recess. The dining tables were each covered in linen and then lacquered, giving the tables a fine mesh finish. *Tatami* mats are spread across the floor. Meanwhile, the walls are coated in a sand mix, to give a light texturing, which was coloured using powdered seaweed, washing the restaurant in a gentle green hue.

The carefully selected materials and the way each has been treated provide diners with an exquisitely tactile, understated setting which is ideal for perfectly prepared dishes of vinegared rice rolls dipped in ginger or wasabi.

A Residence with Louvres
That Form a Filter between Public
and Private Spaces

T-house (an abbreviation of the clients' surname) is a residence built on a plot located in Kobe's densely built up central business district near Shin-Kobe Station. The clients, a young, 30-something couple, approached Intentionallies with a plot of land measuring just 4 m wide and 10 m deep and a desire for a house that would enable them to enjoy city life more fully. The site had obvious advantages, but it was also afflicted with disadvantages. Although buildings were located on both sides of the plot, meaning side windows were not an option, the site received lots of natural light. However, the reason the site was well lit was because the area in front of the south-facing façade was open, as it contained a road. At over 20 m wide, the road was extremely busy during peak commute times, resulting in considerable noise and air pollution from the heavy traffic.

As space was limited, Intentionallies developed a design scheme with higher than usual ceilings, to provide space to install additional volumes as mezzanines. Two functions were located on each of the four floors. On the ground floor was the entrance and garage; on the first floor, a bedroom and bathroom; on the second floor, a living room, dining room and kitchen, plus a deck area. The third floor contained a second bedroom and a storage space. A flight of stairs connected the floors. As the site was so narrow, locating the stairs to the rear of the house was an option, rather than have the stairwell cut into the already limited floor space in the core of the house. However, Intentionallies chose to locate the staircase in the heart of the house. The firm also installed a long skylight in the ceiling over the stairwell on the top floor, to bring natural light into the house. To ensure sufficient daylight could filter down through the house, the firm designed stairs for the top two sections that resembled the louvres installed in the windows on each floor, so sunlight spills down through the stair section of the house. An appealing side effect is the play of light that changes according to the time of day.

The buildings flanking T-house are taller than the four-storey house. To counter any feelings of being hemmed in, Intentionallies set out to create interiors with as big a view of the cityscape outside as the space permitted. The firm achieved this by installing glazed walls in the façade. On the first floor, the glazed area starts at hip height, but on the second and third floors, the glazed walls are floor-to-ceiling as well as wall-to-wall. However, the proximity to the road meant protection was needed to minimize the traffic noise. To meet this challenge, Shuwa Tei installed three sliding doors, fitted with wooden louvres, on the exterior of each floor on the south facing side of the house overlooking the road. The density of the slats in each of the louvres differed: the left-hand panel was the most dense, the right-hand panel the least, and the middle panel a mid-way between the two. The louvres formed a filter between the house and the urban environment outside, providing a screen for privacy as much as for noise. The louvres operate on a sliding mechanism, letting light in while shielding the interiors from too much sun when necessary. The light filtering through the slats creates an attractive moiré pattern on the floor and across the interior of each storey.

Intentionallies selected a steel-framed structure for the house, to maximize the interior floor space. Despite the narrow plot, the supporting walls of the building had to be stand alone for anti-seismic reasons, and so are set in from the walls of neighbouring buildings, in accordance with Japanese building law. A number of 10 cm² pillars were placed in the interior walls of the stairwell while, on the exterior, 25 cm² columns support the roof slabs. Solid wood was used for the flooring and the external walls consist of compressed plastic cement board.

The densely populated city environment is one of the principal features of urban living, both now and in the future. Although people dwelling in such locations can find day-to-day events stressful, most of the time this can be countered by intelligent design. Says Shuwa Tei, 'We find that designing a structure from the innermost details to the exterior enables us to influence the impact of the surrounding city on the site. We embrace elements that are desirable, and screen out those which are less desirable.' In fact, the design of T-house is coming to be accepted as the epitome of collected thinking, and it is a tacit indication of the possibility of extending the architecture of a single unit to that of an entire city.

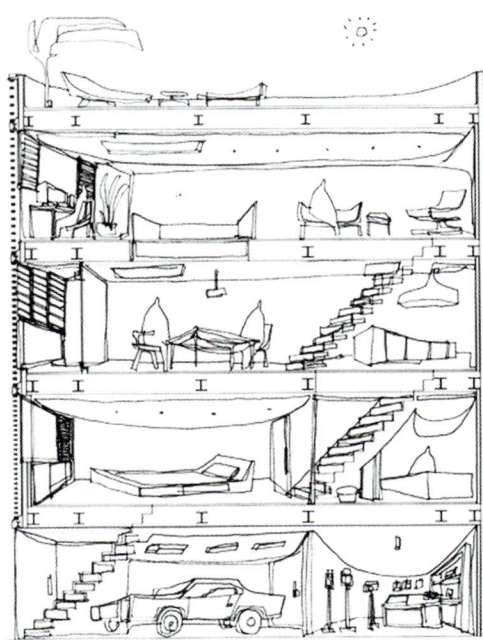

Intentionallies   At Home in Tokyo

Speeding up the Ageing Process of Materials

Intentionallies was commissioned to rejuvenate the terrace of a house in Tokyo's Harajuku district that had been built 25 years earlier. The client, Mr Endo, had lived in Sri Lanka for a period where he'd been inspired by an architect he'd met, Geoffrey Bawa, who had taken an interest in tropical modernism. Bawa had played with the ageing of materials, placing freshly cut stone in a lake or river for a month before using it to build with, so the material no longer looked new. Inspired by Bawa, Intentionallies experimented with the treatment of the materials to be used on the roof garden. A corridor leading out to the terrace was to be laid with sandstone. As Intentionallies didn't have the freedom (or climate) that Bawa'd had, living on an island, the firm investigated alternative approaches like watering freshly cut stone with a hose. Over the course of a year, Intentionallies found that using a hose on the stone over an extended period aged the stone, achieving an effect that was similar to Bawa's. Intentionallies covered other materials in soil for a month. When dug up, the cold feel had been shed and replaced with a warmer patina. Speeding up the process of acquiring a history ensured the terrace looked as if it had been established many years earlier, just as the client desired.

A Building with a Footprint Defined by Its Neighbours

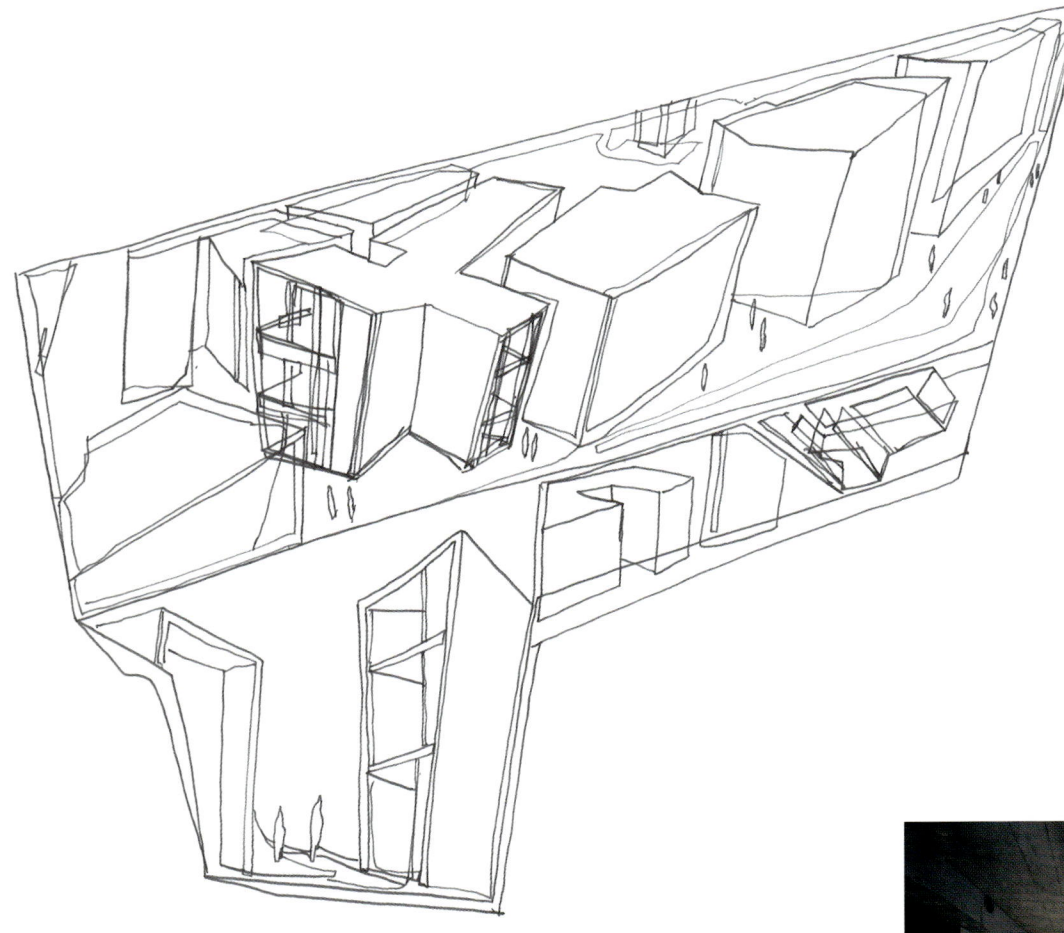

Intentionallies | At Home in Tokyo

When commissioned to design an office block in Jingumae, Tokyo, Intentionallies was faced with the challenge of an awkwardly shaped site. Almost a rhombus, but with a chunk taken out of it, the plot 'resembled a hairdryer or a hand gun', says Shuwa Tei. 'We could have constructed a building with a more regular, rectangular footprint,' adds Tei, 'But the client required the maximum floor space possible for the offices.' Intentionallies' solution was to allow the building's immediate neighbours and the local construction regulations – which stipulated the minimum distance permitted between buildings – to define the profile of the offices. The result is an angular block with no fewer than nine sides, each connected to the next by a sharp arris. It slots perfectly into – and all but fills – the void left by the surrounding buildings. Its rear façade is stepped and has three faces but it is the front façade that is the showstopper. It features a soaring wall of glass with a twisted perspective, where the supporting wall to the left is set a few metres back from that on the right. The building is finished in black concrete, which was polished to create a glossy finish. Highlighting the dramatic outline is a fluorescent band that follows the contour of the main façade. The stripe is made up of tiles, co-developed by Intentionallies, that absorb light by day and store it, until darkness falls, when the body of the building disappears, leaving a soft, green line glowing in the night.

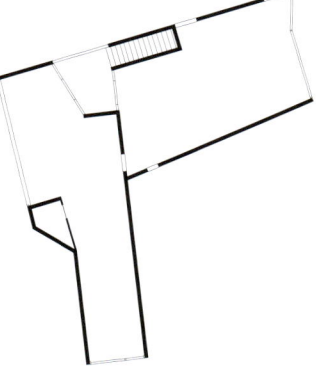

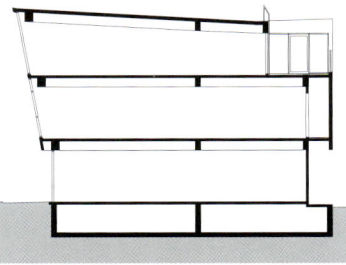

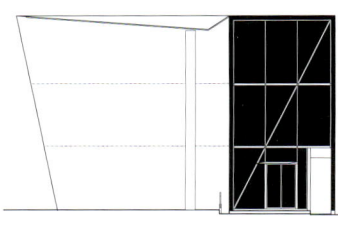

A Two-family Dwelling

A two-family residence for clients in their mid-30s and the parents of one of the pair, Shelton's house is located in a quiet, secluded Tokyo neighbourhood near Shinjuku. Intentionallies' challenge was to insert the dwelling into an ordinary residential area made up of two-storey buildings. In order to define the structure in the context of its surroundings, Shuwa Tei had to decide whether or not to employ architectural techniques that would open up the house to the street. Together with the client, Intentionallies opted for a scheme that closes the house to the street in front of it.

The resulting residence has a façade that is an imposing concrete wall, with not one window in the sheer face presented to the road. To give both the young couple and the older parents a sense of independence, Intentionallies constructed two entrances. One is accessed on the left of the reinforced concrete façade. The other is to the right, set slightly back, where a prism-shaped volume was extracted from the right-hand side of the house, just behind the façade. The void created a mini-courtyard where a window inserted in the back wall allows an oblique view onto the road, and an entrance is given a self-contained feel. Inside the house, in marked contrast to the façade, the interiors are very open. The stairs seem to float, thanks to elegant treads neatly fixed into the concrete wall of the stairwell. Wooden flooring and decking – laid on the terrace on the top floor – add warmer tones to the greys of the concrete walls. From within, with just a sliver of the cityscape visible, the house demonstrates how its architecture and the surrounding neighbourhood can be visually connected.

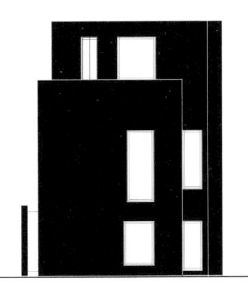

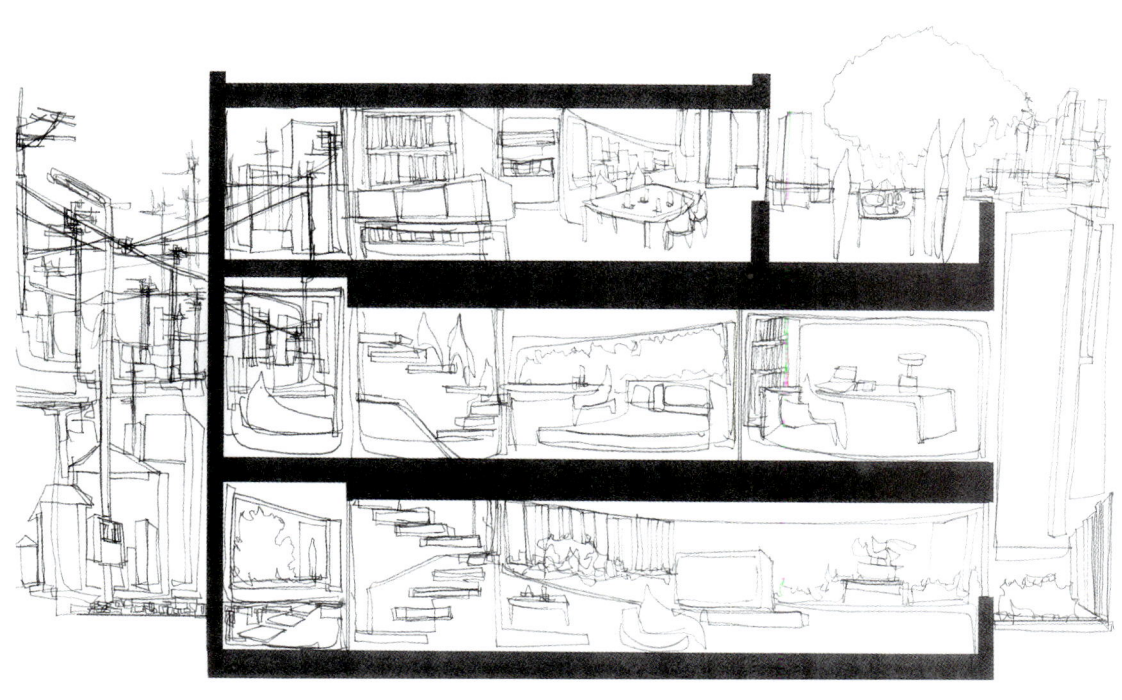

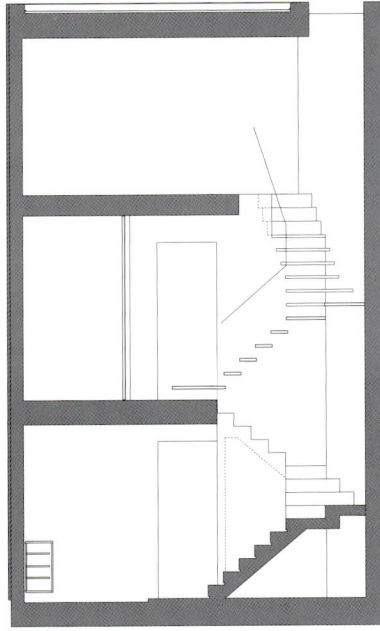

The Beauty of Japan

One aspect of design is taking ancient traditions and techniques and reinventing them, giving them a new value. Shuwa Tei explains, 'It's creating meaning anew. Traditions must evolve. Linking state-of-the-art technology to the newest developments must be made a priority. Continuity then has the possibility of becoming a tradition in the future, of becoming a classic.' Tei continues, 'I have taken the industrial art of the 20th century and reinterpreted it with today's sense of beauty, expressing it in terms of today's Japan. I have been inspired by objects and events from history and woven them into objects and spaces we've designed. Although a standard design language exists, and is used throughout the world, I consider traditional beauty and an appreciation of the four seasons a vital component to design.'

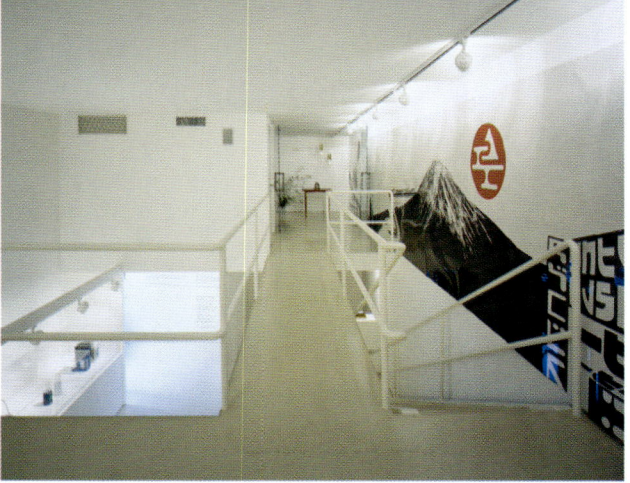

An Exhibition With a Japanese Context

At the Salone Internazionale del Mobile in Milan in 2005, Intentionallies exhibited furniture and lighting created in-house, in addition to products from the amadana line. The amadana collection was received with such enthusiasm a new Japanese word was coined, *caden*, to describe the fresh approach the firm had taken in the home appliances field. Intentionallies also designed the layout of the exhibition, setting the pieces off against a backdrop that was a fusion between hi tech and traditional Japanese elements, placing the objects in context.

Bringing Sensor Technology and Japanese Aesthetics Together in One Exhibit

Intentionallies designed an exhibition for TOTO that appeared at the 100% Design Tokyo event in 2008 in Shibuya. Intentionallies' presentation was also one of four selected to represent TOTO in 2009 at ISH Frankfurt, a trade show for bathroom solutions. The exhibit was an integral part of TOTO's endeavour to expand the brand in Europe. Intentionallies observed that TOTO, a market leader in sensor technology, attached a great deal of importance to water and cleanliness, and did so in a typically Japanese way. In addition, the firm was clearly proud of its association with traditional Japanese art.

Intentionallies brought Japanese aesthetics to the fore in the exhibition, using water and light to present the brand's products. An interactive sensor mechanism, designed by TOTO, was put in place so that visitors' footsteps would trigger ripple-like light patterns to appear on the floor, as though the visitor was walking through water. The ripple effect spread across the floor of the stand. The wow factor was magnified by strategically placed mirrors that reflected the water patterns further. The installation enabled visitors to experience TOTO's technological competence firsthand, and showcased the inventive and creative possibilities offered by the firm's sensors.

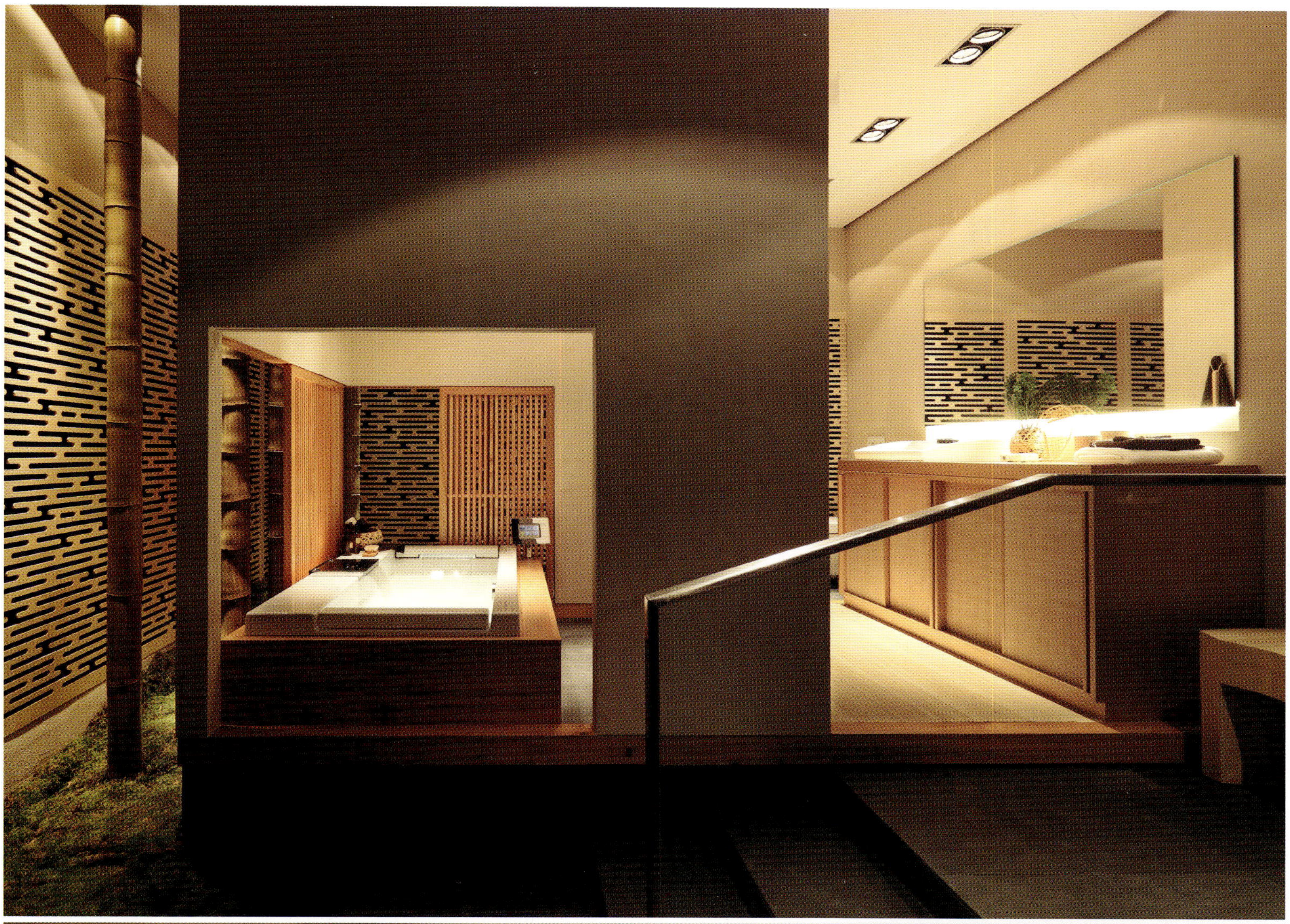

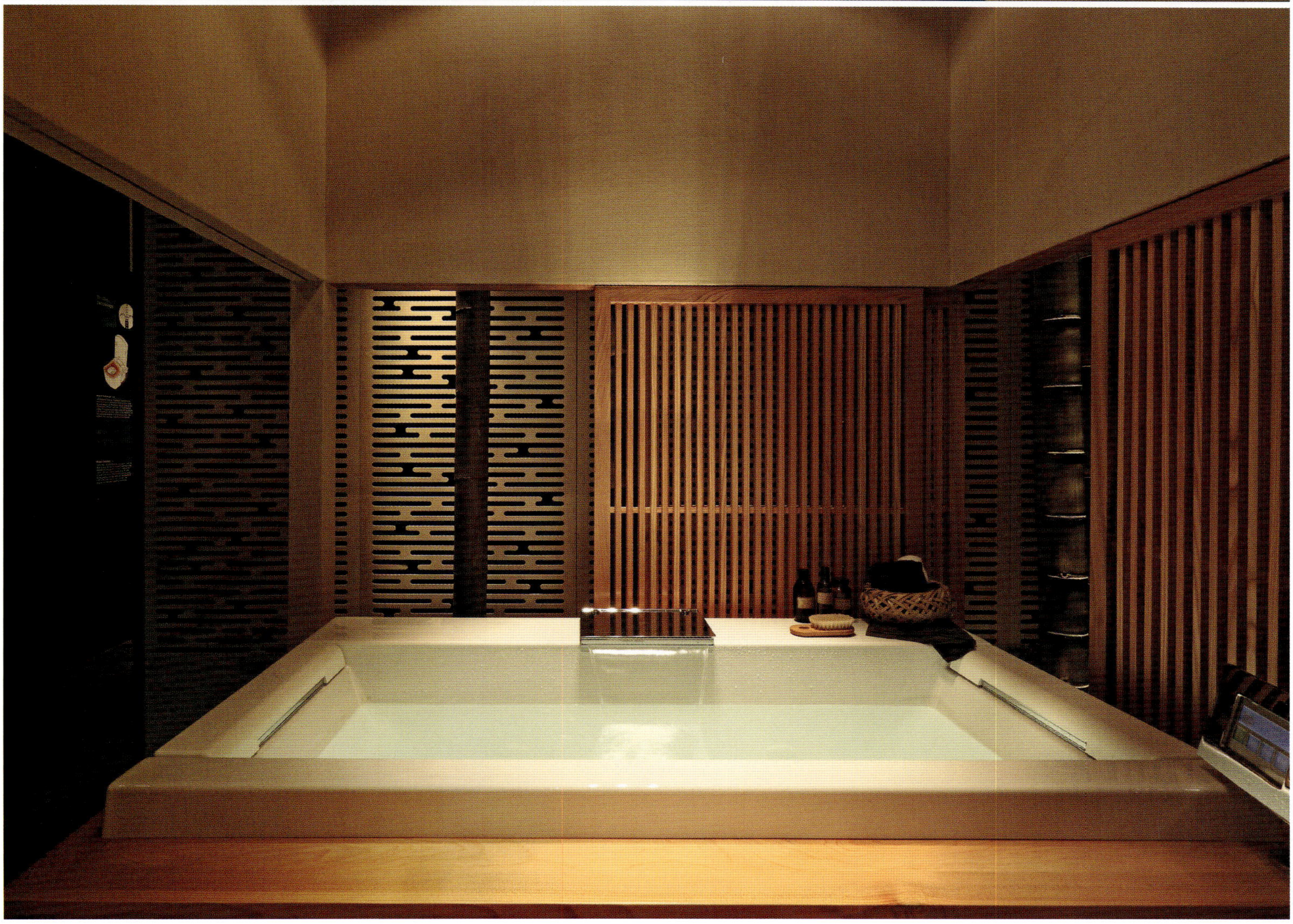

A Shop That Reflects Its Collection

A shop defines, to an extent, the collection of products it showcases. Several years ago, the amadana line was launched with a range of products designed by Realfleet, the firm that Tei had founded in 2002 with two former Toshiba employees to design electronics. The products were developed under strict aesthetic principles and the resulting line of home appliances stood out from competitors thanks to the elegant lines and profiles of the products. In the process of shaping amadana into a general home appliances brand, the firm came to realize that the space where products are displayed was as vital, in terms of the impact made on shoppers, as the products themselves.

In 2006, a dedicated store called amadana Omotesando Hills opened in Tokyo's Shibuya district. The design concept behind the amadana line was for each product to project its own design qualities onto its surroundings and to represent a subtractive approach to design, so all imperfections were removed and each item was distilled to its core elements. The space is not only a shop, but it also adds depth to the customer's shopping experience by reflecting the qualities that define the amadana collection itself.

amadana Omotesando Hills

The Beauty of Japan

Intentionallies

amadana Nakameguro

amadana Ginza

A sense of four seasons with leaving its marginal space intentionally

The first restaurant project that Intentionallies worked on was Hanamiduki, located in Tokyo's Jingumae district. It was completed in 1999. The studio was entirely responsible for the planning and interior design of the restaurant, and its furnishings. The project was also the first that Intentionallies approached holistically, with the firm addressing the uniform worn by the restaurant staff and the dishes served. Shuwa Tei explains that, 'Nothing is more important than clothing, food and shelter because they are the basics needed for survival.'

For Hanamiduki, Intentionallies set out to express the essence of Japan, namely the qualities that initially appear simple, but are actually rich in substance and dignified style. Tei elaborates: 'At Intentionallies, we see space as something that continuously evolves. We don't view it as a finished, permanent state. To this end, when we choose furnishings, we select elements that change continuously, so the space can develop over time, evolving in tandem with the seasons. At Hanamiduki, the chair and table heights and the configuration of the planes were determined by how much of the surrounding scenery we wanted to open up to the diners.' The firm ensured that the garden, furnished with what are rather poetically called moon-viewing benches, did not conflict with interior furnishings and views were not blocked by, for example, vases of flowers. The result is an integrated composition that is pleasing to the eye.

Intentionallies extended the renovation to the restaurant's menu, collaborating with local and international specialists from a range of backgrounds to craft seasonal foodie delights. Says Tei, 'We've striven to craft something new and to balance that with an atmosphere that is cocooning, nostalgic even, to maintain an all important harmony.'

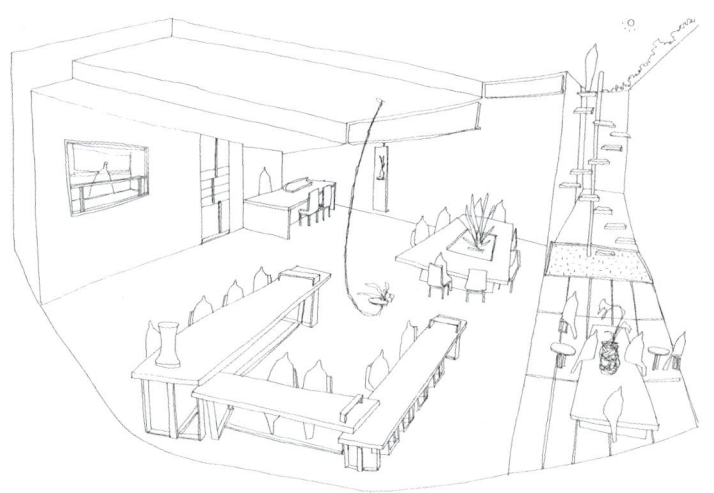

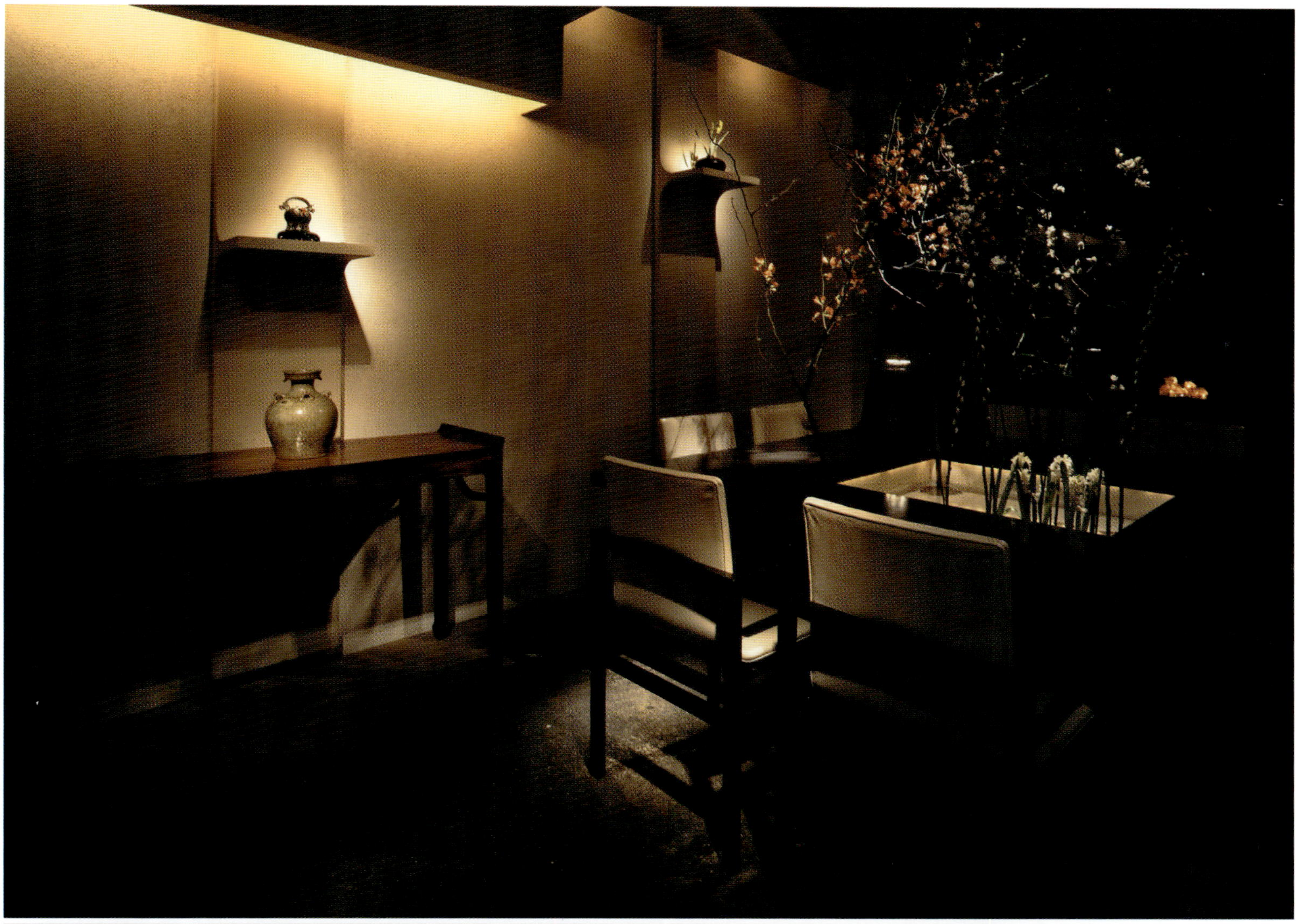

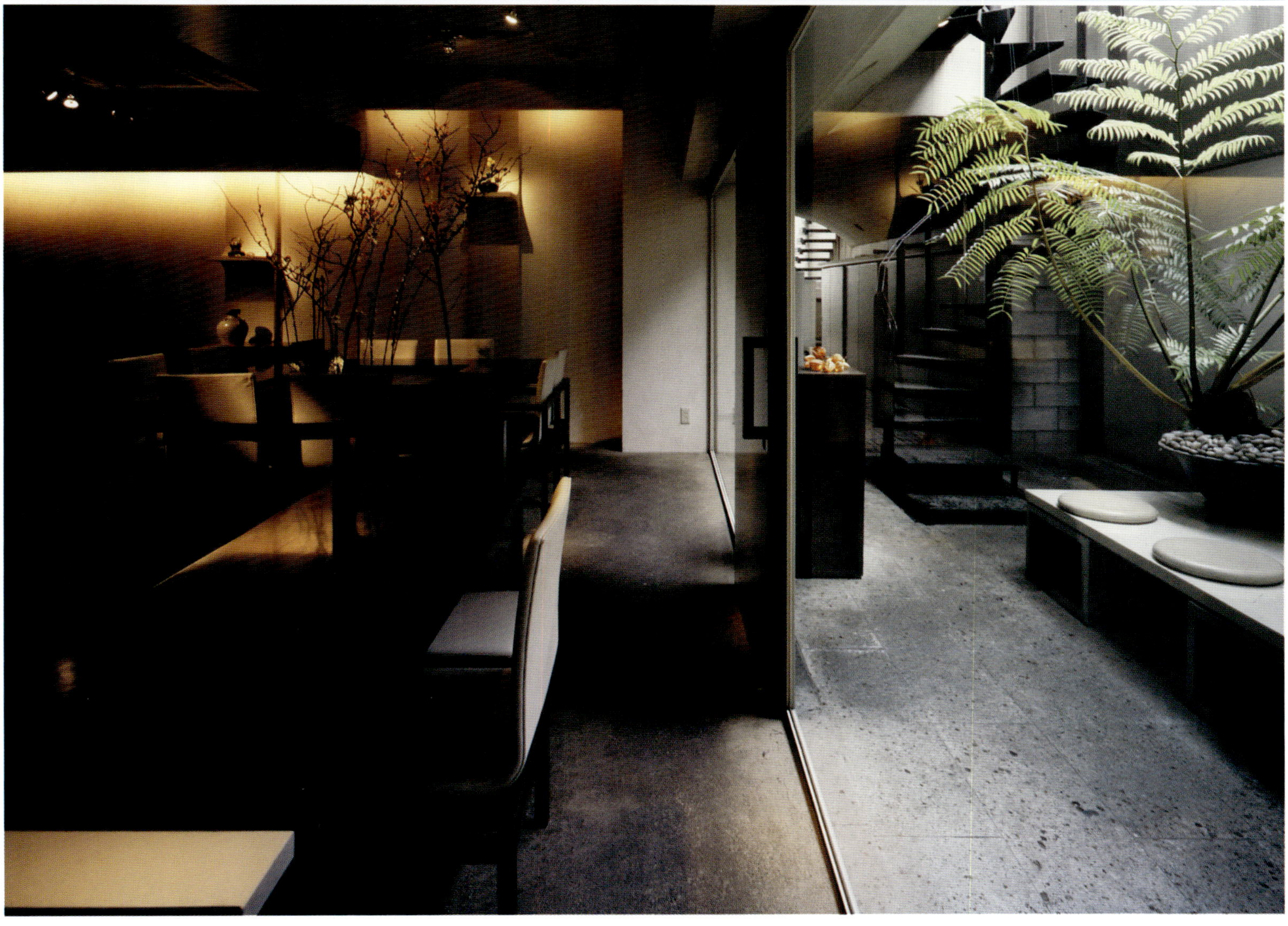

The Beauty of Japan

Intentionallies

The Architecture of Space / Atmosphere

What is meant by the description stylishly dignified? Shuwa Tei comments, 'I often think about this. It is not something that can be attributed to history, status, value, reputation or genre. It transcends drawings and computer graphics. It is quite simply intrinsic to a space, one that feels fresh and new but is nonetheless comforting. The way materials and furnishings are handled plays a vital role in the overall stylishly dignified nature of a space.

Architecture and interiors are anchored in their location. We consider the relationship between a site and its culture, history and the context of the location to be of the utmost importance. When devising a solution, we continually search for that elusive, stylishly dignified quality as we shape the atmosphere, wrapping each space in subtle, delicate details while erasing all traces of our labour to ensure the result is effortless.'

Providing Patients With a Comforting Clinic

When commissioned to design a private ear, nose and throat clinic for a client in Osaka, Intentionallies set out to create a spa-like atmosphere, to offer patients a more calming environment than the standard medical facility, which can be cold and uninviting. Although Intentionallies had just 160 m² to work with, the firm made the most of the available space by ensuring each square metre was used as efficiency as possible. Intentionallies created a comforting reception area by using paint in warm pink tones with soft lighting overhead. Even the reception desk was a dusky pink. The choice of wooden furniture and flooring throughout ensured the clinic and the consultation rooms carried an inviting air. The effect of using white ash or walnut on its own would have resulted in a space that was too stark, so Intentionallies used both, balancing them against the reddish hues of ironwood, which added extra warmth.

Extending the Walls of a House to Frame an Incredible View

Intentionallies was brought in to build a holiday house in the foothills of the Yatsugatake Mountains. The plot of land was one of five with planning permission. Although the other sites hadn't been developed, Intentionallies factored future neighbours into the concept to ensure the clients retained their privacy. The defining element of the design was however, determined by the impressive view. With the Yatsugatake Mountain range to the north and Mount Fuji and the Southern Alps visible to the south, Shuwa Tei designed the house to frame the view of the landscape. Because of the gently sloping ground, the house doesn't have conventional foundations, but instead rests on cantilevers. From a distance, the construction appears to float just above the ground. Raising the house also brought the occupants even better views of the surroundings. The wooden house faces south, and has an extensive deck on the south side. Two parallel walls extend southwards on either side of the building. The same height as the top of the roof, the walls flank the deck, creating an open-fronted, open-topped enclosure. The construction frames the panorama unfolding to the south while shielding the house and deck area from any buildings that may appear in the future, maintaining the clients' privacy and preventing the magnificent view from being impaired. The view also dictated the layout of the interior. Inside the house, sandwiched between the east and west walls and facing south, is the living room. Its orientation towards the view ensures it is bathed in the maximum amount of sunlight, making it an optimal choice for the family's main living space.

The Architecture of Space / Atmosphere

Intentionallies

Crafting a Balance Between Materials, Hospitality and Functional Fixtures

Strasburgo Osaka

When Italian firm Strasburgo opened its first store in Osaka offering custom-made suits, it was seen as something of a pioneer, as bespoke tailoring was not common in Japan. Intentionallies was brought in to extend the brand's Osaka shop, where a newly acquired first floor was to be integrated into the existing ground floor space. In addition to made-to-measure Italian suits, the store also sold select, high-quality labels, imported from Europe. To reflect the finely finished clothing stocked, the client asked Intentionallies for a high level of craftsmanship throughout the store.

Intentionallies responded with a mix of materials, carefully chosen to shape the atmosphere desired. For a display wall, the firm worked and treated leather – employing the same techniques used to prepare the materials for pieces in the clothing collections – before applying it to the wall. Elsewhere, for a different wall finish, Intentionallies took inspiration from Le Corbusier, who used wood moulds to obtain a grain-like surface in concrete. Intentionallies, however, reinterpreted the procedure. The wall panelling in the store is actually made of cedar that has been sandblasted to bring out the texture of the grain. After being treated to several coats of paint, the surface has a concrete-like appearance, creating an effect very like Le Corbusier's. Concrete also features in the space, as the stairs between the two floors were made from moulded concrete with integrated lighting set under each tread. Origami-inspired pendant lamps that are made from paper add a deft, structured touch overhead. Shuwa Tei explains, 'We used solid materials, not just surface finishes, as we required the interior to have a feeling of depth and honesty.'

Strasburgo Aoyama

Intentionallies also installed carefully crafted materials in the Strasburgo store in Aoyama, where it was equally important that the aesthetic behind the brand mirrored the shop interior. At just 66 m², the store was not large, but the client requested a dedicated space where clients could be welcomed with a coffee, and given the time and attention required for tailor-made clothing, where choices span every variable right down to the thread used. Intentionallies established a one-to-one area, referred to as the salon, where elegant sofas and armchairs provide the space to discuss tailoring options.

As the first Strasburgo branch to feature tailored womenswear as well as menswear, the Aoyama store featured merchandizing displays that had a light touch. Structured entirely in glass, the shelving systems were crafted from bonded glass. Shuwa Tei explains, 'It's usually difficult to ensure the bond connection is also clear glass, but as we didn't want the frame in a different material, we made sure it worked.' The flooring is Japanese walnut, instead of the darker standard walnut. The lighter hue of the wood brought out a variety of grains, adding rich tones to the space. A louvre-like system of multifunctional sliding doors includes fittings where shoppers can hang selected items as they browse. In the changing rooms, wooden wall panelling was originally flooring, which was recycled to great effect. An additional, significant feature of the shop is that the display elements are movable and so can be tucked out of sight in the storage area when the shop is required to function as an event space. While the palette of colours in the Aoyama shop is coordinated with the tones of the Osaka shop, an independent identity is clearly established in each of the two stores through a subtle variation in the materials used.

A Verdant Interior for an Underground Store

Intentionallies' concept for a retail store in Shibuya was inspired by the notions of a designer's atelier and a *maison*. The space is characterized by banks of bushy tropical plants installed on either side of a clothing rack, creating a verdant, symmetrical display. The greenery gives the store – which is actually located underground – a fresh, outdoorsy feeling, while the rich hues imbue the shop with a shot of glamour. The atmosphere fulfils the objective Intentionallies set, which was to add an unexpected element to the space, bringing the brand's uniqueness to the fore. Wooden flooring and objects made of stone add to the nature-associated aesthetic. In addition, the two fitting rooms both have interesting ceilings. One is equipped with an infinity mirror and the other with a mirror ball. The changing rooms, where – the label hopes – a transformation quite literally takes place, serve to bring fresh perspectives to customers.

Using Textiles in a Spa to Wrap Clients in Comfort

Where and how a person relaxes is as integral to leisure time as the active entertainments chosen. This does not only apply to Tokyo-ites, but to most affluent urban dwellers. When Intentionallies was brought in to craft a spa in a space occupying 182 m² in Shibuya, the firm was keen to craft an atmosphere that enveloped clients in a comfortable, calming tone. The concept was apt as the name of the spa, Fango, is Italian for mud, and hints at the treatments – like a mud wrap, for example – on offer to clients. Although the ceiling was low at 2.2 m – the space had previously been used for offices – Intentionallies transformed the potential negative into a defining characteristic of the spa, that of intimacy. Intentionallies used several different textiles in the space. Instead of wallpaper, the firm applied linen to the walls, and used slim planks of walnut to frame each section of the beige fabric. The richly coloured, shiny curtains that are drawn to give clients privacy provide a contrast in materials. Intentionallies built each treatment bed to provide storage. Incorporated into the walnut base are pullout drawers providing space for the electrical equipment required for specific treatments. Tucking the equipment out of sight when not in use ensures the treatment room retains an uncluttered, calming aura. Ceiling spotlights washing the space in a gentle glow are adjustable, so for a particularly intense treatment, the beauty technician can dim the lights to envelope the client in an extra calming atmosphere.

Intentionallies' use of materials was sophisticated. The firm used natural materials in soothing neutral shades, the creams, tans and deep greens evoking an association with nature, a subtle reminder of the products used in the spa.

Lighting For a Café

Intentionallies was asked to create a café in the middle of Umeda, a town near Osaka, that blended in with its surroundings. The firm set out to give visitors to the café the impression that far from being brand new, it was well established. The objective was achieved by ensuring that that the design did not overwhelm, and instead, was subtle. The space was also comfortable with a long-lasting appeal. The signature element in the café is a series of pendant lamps whose form was inspired by the traditional Japanese art of origami. Each of the nine lamps has a profile that looks somewhat familiar, in a comforting way, without being overly distracting. Intentionallies was pleased with the result, as the lamps attract a degree of curiosity that gives an accent to the space.

A Finely-crafted Restaurant Inspired by Sumo Cuisine

Kita No Fuji is a very popular restaurant located in Hokkaido that specializes in serving *chanko*, a stew commonly eaten by sumo wrestlers. A one-pot dish, *chanko* is a chicken broth with large quantities of chicken, fish, tofu or beef added, along with vegetables like bok choy. When the owner of the eatery decided open a *chanko* restaurant in Tokyo, called Chanko dining Sakurai, Intentionallies was commissioned to shape the space. The owner requested the philosophy behind the creation of the dish was displayed prominently in the restaurant.

Intentionallies positioned a giant stockpot just inside the entrance of the main restaurant space. With a diameter of 2 m, the pot is the first thing that clients see on climbing the stairs and coming into the first floor space. In addition, the symbolic pot is visible to passersby in the street, as the vessel can be clearly seen from the pavement, thanks to the glazed walls that wrap the restaurant. Although it is set behind a glass display case, the pot is not only a revered exhibit, but it is actually heated and used to make *chanko*. The presentation backs onto the kitchen so the culinary team, who have access to the steaming pot via a curtain to the rear of the display, can take servings of the stew or add more ingredients through the evening. By giving the active showcase such a central position, Intentionallies provided diners with an iconic reminder of the restaurant's speciality dish. In addition, using a utensil – which would usually never leave the kitchen – as decoration also added a light-hearted note.

Sandstone flanks the wall nearest the pot. Engraved by hand into the stone are symbols inspired by traditional sumo images that Intentionallies developed with a graphic designer. In the centre of the restaurant is an enormous table made from two planks sliced from a colossal tree trunk. Overhead are generously sized lampshades featuring an original pattern that is a modern take on the traditional *kumiko* where small pieces of wood are assembled to create intricate latticework.

By focusing on a select number of large-scale objects, Intentionallies has created a restaurant that gives diners a strong sense of the history of the cuisine on offer. That said, even though the installations are an impressive size, they do not distract attention from the enjoyment of the food.

An Open-air Rooftop Restaurant

Intentionallies was commissioned to craft a restaurant on the roof of a building that housed an apparel shop in Tokyo. The space, called Tabayatei, began life as a members-only restaurant for the clothing brand. The top floor site already contained a building suitable for a kitchen, and a wide terrace. Protecting the terrace from inclement weather was an elegant glass roof that arched down from the top of the kitchen structure to the floor of the terrace. Intentionallies renovated the roofing and in the process, replaced the glass panels with fabric that can be rolled up, like a blind, to create an almost open-air dining experience. Long rows of tables and chairs are neatly arranged under the cloth canopy. The menu offers a fusion between Japanese cuisine and select dishes from across Asia. A separate zone, outside the covered area, provides diners waiting for a table with seating.

An Interior Divided to Accommodate Two Households

Kimura's house is a residential project located in Shinagawa, in Tokyo's greater metropolitan area. When complete, the three-storey house, which also has one floor underground, was destined to become home to two households comprising four generations ranging in age from four to 95. Included in the group was a wife and her mother-in-law. The assignment was challenging. The plot was small but the client requested sufficient private space for each of the two women so that the two branches of the family could live together. Intentionallies responded to the brief by giving each family its own front door. Next, instead of constructing the house in one block and dedicating the rear of the plot to a garden, Intentionallies created a central courtyard. The void forms a natural break and separates the house into two sections. The two households can operate independently, but family members can get together in the courtyard, generating a positive atmosphere for all concerned. From the street, the reinforced concrete façade blends discretely in with the neighbouring houses, with no indication that the house within is divided, so the family's private business remains private.

The Ageing of Buildings Brings out the Beauty of The Materials

A three-building complex located on a woody slope near Lake Haruna, northwest of Tokyo, was completed in 2001. The clients, a Tokyo-based couple, planned to move to the house once they had retired, when the residence would become their permanent home. Despite the fact that inclement weather sees temperatures dropping to -10C in winter, the site was specially chosen. The local land was protected: the forestry authorities imposed restrictions forbidding the sale of plots measuring less than 1,000 m² and logging is also limited, factors that ensured the preservation of the surrounding environment. The clients requested a house built with the philosophical simplicity of 'The Ten Foot Square Hut', a reference to a thoughtful essay by a Buddhist priest that is representative of the literature of the reclusive genre. The clients, more than anything else, wanted a site for peaceful meditation.

The plot is extensive, but Intentionallies opted for several smaller buildings rather than one large construction to minimize the impact on the landscape, as the area had to be cleared of trees before building began, and the clients didn't want to fell any more than was absolutely necessary. The three-building complex comprises the main house, a library – the couple are academics and have a lot of books – and a shed used principally for storing firewood. Dividing the structure also made sense ecologically, as each was tailored to the function it fulfilled. The main house and the library did not, for example, require the same level of insulation, enabling the insulation in the latter to be scaled back to the bare level required for the space to function. Although not the largest building of the complex, the library was considered the core of the project as it took on an almost sacred feel, as it was not merely a storage space for books, but was a dedicated area for the clients to retreat to, from the main house, to relax.

The firm was much concerned with the challenge of incorporating the house into the slope of the land and the necessary countermeasures needed to take the one-metre freeze depth of the soil into consideration. The most direct approach would have been to create an artificial base that separated the building from the sloping ground by raising it on piers, a method of coping with the geographic features that the client requested from Intentionallies. However, in order to build a large house on a steeply sloping site it would have been necessary to excavate a large amount of soil. Intentionallies reduced

this to a minimum, firstly by selecting a site on the plot with the smallest angle of slope and secondly by dividing the various areas of the buildings into mezzanines on different levels. Excavation could be further reduced by backfilling an area of ground equivalent to the area excavated, providing a level platform on which to build. However, it was essential to reduce the difference in floor levels between the mezzanines as much as possible, given that the house was meant for an elderly couple.

A Nordic approach was the inspiration for the profile of the main house and the planning of the interior layout. The building is in the form of a penthouse with a sloping roof in a natural form that takes in the light and wind effectively on the northern side of the slope and allows snow to fall naturally from the roof. The interior of the house features elements common to Scandinavian housing, for example, a wood burning stove.

Each building is crafted from materials that at first glance seem to be of a similar composition, but which will in fact, says Shuwa Tei, 'Weather and mature at different rates.' Tei continues, 'The rain that helps plants to grow also stimulates the evolution of the buildings.' The exterior of the main building was constructed from Japanese cedar and over time, its patina will become more mature, and the change to the material will be visible. Part of the exterior of the library was flanked in copper panels. Over time, the copper will be covered in a green patina, or verdigris. Meanwhile, the flat-roofed woodshed was covered in a louvre-like woven system. Set behind the main house, it fitted so seamlessly into the woodland context of the site that it was almost camouflaged. Intentionallies wanted to make a clear separation between the three buildings in the complex, so while it was apparent the structures were related, the design and finish of each was independent.

The inevitable ageing of buildings is one of the considerations that designers have to take into account. Various factors cause this ageing such as the natural environment and the usage of the building and also the blending in of repairs and replacements that become necessary over the longer term. This process can bring out the beauty of the materials in a building that deserves to last for a long time. Shuwa Tei adds, 'The buildings will each express the passage of time in a profoundly different way.' He concludes, 'The independent life of the project began the moment the construction was complete.'

A Set of Showrooms Providing Interior Solutions for a Range of Styles

Intentionallies was asked by a company that specializes in DIY tools to design a showroom for a newly opened branch of a firm that dealt with minor renovations. The client asked for a series of different spaces within the showroom to demonstrate different concepts. Intentionallies devised an interior style system that could be applied to any room in a house. 'You read the system like a chart,' says Shuwa Tei. There are three alternative styles for each room. 'There's a modern monotone version that does not have a great variety of materials, there's a very warm comfortable version, with lots of different woods for example, and one that falls between the two.' The three presentations have the same functions, but feature different materials, details and finishes, so customers can see what each space would look like after being renovated in the specific style. There are also systems designed for multi-family units. Shuwa Tei concludes, 'We redefined each space as a functional, appealing interior, presenting a systematic set of solutions for clients living in Tokyo.'

Communication / Collaboration

In demonstrating concepts for a building design, for either the exterior or the interior, it is impractical to show it full scale. Shuwa Tei elaborates, saying, 'If you could, that would be ideal. You can, however, use models, two-dimensional graphics or design sketches, but there is definitely a gap between those and the real thing. In using these techniques there is scope for the views of colleagues to be considered. It is not a question of right or wrong; sometimes we complete the design, sometimes we leave parts blank. We are particularly conscious at this stage that we are communicating with each other, therefore we don't rely on established means, rather, we are constantly searching for new methods of communication.'

Tei continues, 'Intentionallies starts from the premise that, while something can be planned and designed by one person, it cannot be made by one person, but we do not stop there. We believe that it is very beneficial to collaborate enthusiastically to learn new things of new value. This collaboration involves not only graphic designers, web designers and artists but it also extends to craftsmen who have traditional knowledge and skills, learned scholars from other fields, research facilities with specialized technologies, talented engineers and other professionals. Our objective is to constantly aim for the optimum solution and to produce something of the highest value. There are no rules or established methods for achieving this: we always approach a problem with an open mind and with determination to find the best possible solution.'

Seamlessly Connected Interiors for a New Fashion Label

Motion Element Aoyama

Intentionallies was brought in as a consultant to work on the branding for the new fashion label Motion Element, and to craft the store interiors. Intentionallies collaborated with a graphic firm to produce the logo and graphics for the brand. The first store to be completed was in Aoyama. Behind a soaring glass façade is a series of spaces that are all connected by a clothing rail that runs, uninterrupted, through each retail zone in the three-storey shop. Adding to the seamless feel were the fixtures and fittings, all of which were created by Intentionallies. Etched into the interior panes of the glass façade is a bamboo-inspired graphic pattern. The glass has been treated so it appears to be green from the exterior but is almost colourless when looking out. The firm also designed a mahogany chair with a bar-like backrest that cantilevered out from the armrests. The technical form was inspired by the Motion Element logo. Opting to shape the seat from wood proved very challenging, but the rich colour and feel of the material created a warm tone in the space, while giving the chair a lightness that reflected the brand.

Intentionallies   Communication / Collaboration

Motion Element Nagoya

Inspired by an airport lounge, the Motion Element interior that Intentionallies designed for the brand's Nagoya store was located in a shopping mall. The concept behind its construction is similar to that of the Aoyama store, but with an additional dimension, as it was developed as a transitional space. It featured a very open layout, as though it were in an airport lounge, and fixtures and lighting were placed at random to emphasize the spaciousness of the shop floor. The north-facing façade of the store featured glazing treated to look green from the exterior. Acrylic lighting fixtures suspended overhead are an ironic interpretation of fluorescent strip lamps; the lighting in the Nagoya store was given a very polished finish.

Motion Element Marunouchi

Green glass presentation cases characterize the Motion Element store in Marunouchi. Used to display merchandise, the floor standing units are movable, so can be rearranged to form one long display installation, or five individual ones, depending on the layout required. With a wooden base and glazed upper elements, the units are also flexible in terms of how they can be used to display items, as they can be fitted with shelving to showcase folded clothing, or with railings so pieces can be presented on hangers. Intentionallies designed a chair for the store that corresponded to an uplifting feeling associated with Motion Element products. The seat of the chair cantilevers out from a single, centrally positioned leg. With its stainless steel frame and integrated seat and back pad in tan leather, the chair radiates a smart business-like tone, reflecting the office clothing collections sold in store.

Both Shuwa Tei's career and mine began as the bubble economy burst at the end of the 1980s. This forced us to redefine our philosophy towards design and to refocus on our sense of values. In other words, we had to completely change our thought processes and find a fresh, new approach. Since we are from the same generation, I consider Shuwa as a colleague, a friend and one of the creators whom I respect the most. He is a designer who crosses boundaries and approaches every project, even when exploring unknown territories, with the same high level of perfectionism that is truly his own. His energy and his position of aiming for extremes continue to inspire me. These days, designs from Japan and continental Asia have become widely accepted, and I believe Shuwa Tei is one of the contributors whose work represents the beauty of Japanese design. He presents his principles to the world of design in a truly sophisticated way.

As trite as this may seem, even when I asked him about the designs for our new office space, he was kind enough to share his 'secret recipe' and offered some examples of work that he had undertaken in the past. He may give the impression of being aloof and reserved, but in fact he is one of the warmest and most down-to-earth people I know.

Masamichi Katayama
Interior designer, principal of Wonderwall

A White Ribbon-like Wall System Forms a Flexible Visual Merchandizing Display
That Runs Through the Interior of a Streetwear Store

Inserting
a Blurred Purple Line
Into a White Space
to Emphasize the Core
Concept of Colour

An Experiment Where Red Acrylic Was Inserted Into a White Space to Create Dramatic Effect

Enhancing the Appearance of a Cosmetics Brand

The Japanese cosmetics brand RMK sells its products in over a hundred dedicated stores and shop-in-shops worldwide. Desiring a new design language, the brand contacted Intentionallies. The concept was to be unveiled at the RMK flagship store in Aoyama and then rolled out across shops and concession stands in department stores round the globe.

The main requirement was for Intentionallies to retain the identity of RMK, which it did by using the brand's signature shades of grey and white. The client also asked for a visual merchandizing display that emphasized the

nature of the products. As the skin care range comprised a broad palette of colours, Intentionallies crafted display units made of frosted glass in a stainless steel frame, which were set against a white shop interior. In the Aoyama store, each presentation counter was internally lit with adjustable white and yellow bulbs, and selected counters were fitted with a rear panel, also in frosted glass. Stainless steel polished to a mirror shine was also used to frame all the wall-mounted fashion shots and information panels throughout the store. The near-natural lighting ensured that when clients caught glimpses of themselves, their reflection was flattering. Intentionallies designed a chandelier comprising 3,600 wire-suspended Swarovski crystals, forming a glittering mat that celebrated the new look of the store, giving it an injection of glamour and emphasizing its flagship status.

The firm positioned the chandelier near the glazed façade, where it caught the attention of passersby.

The principle difficulties associated with concession stands in department stores concern the limited floor space – typically ranging from 26 m² to 33 m² – and distractions from surrounding shop-in-shops. The family of display units unveiled in the RMK flagship store, which were used in the smaller RMK shop-in-shops, offered a sophisticated presentation solution. The elegant testing counters enticed shoppers to approach the stand to sample the products. The rear panels screened out the external surroundings, ensuring shoppers gave the product in front of them their full attention, no matter how restricted the space.

A Hair Salon With a Façade that Functions as a Beacon

Azura Omotesando is a hair salon on the upper floor of a building located opposite the Aoyama Street exit of the Tokyo Metro. The salon's owners asked Intentionallies to come up with a concept for the hairdresser's that would form the basis of a Japan-wide rollout and would emphasize azura's position as an upscale brand. Hair salons are usually located on the ground floor to attract walk-in clients who drop in for a cut or restyle. As the site was located one floor up, Intentionallies opted for an eye-catching façade that would encourage passersby to make the journey up the short flight of exterior steps to the salon.

Intentionallies glazed the entire front of the salon, so the azura stylists can be seen, from the street below, as they work on clients in the hair-cutting zone. To really grab the attention of passersby, the firm brought in artisans who etched an intricate, geometric pattern onto sheets of acrylic. The panels were then slotted into the double-glazed façade comprising the entry and reception area of the hairdresser's. The installation was carefully assembled so up close each window appeared to be one enormously thick piece of glass with the etching magically suspended in the middle. The two-

way installation provided an ornamental focus for clients both as they approached via the stairs, and while waiting in the reception area. Horizontal bars of light illuminated the work after dark, creating effective signage advertising the salon. Even at night, when the salon was empty, the styling space was lit so it glowed, lantern-like, alongside the blue installation. Bars of light also featured in the salon's interior where, in the hair-cutting area, the lamps flanked wall-mounted, stainless steel panels that had been polished to a mirror finish.

The custom-designed furniture Intentionallies crafted for the space advanced an aspect that was integral to the concept, which was the importance of comfort, something not frequently associated with chairs in hairdressing salons. A wide chair with armrests and a supportive back pad provided clients with the ideal seat to relax in.

Intentionallies capitalized on what could have been a difficult location and transformed azura Omotesando into a beacon. The firm's solution for the project offers the clients a blueprint that can be adapted to fit further salons in the network.

Booths to Provide Salon Clients With Privacy

Blanco Casual, a hairdressing salon for a young clientele, asked Intentionallies for a space that would appeal to the brand's target group. Located in Harajuku, a district buzzing with young Tokyoites, the space was large enough to accommodate a lot of clients at once, many of whom would be expected to have a quick cut or restyle, so turnover would be rapid, resulting in considerable client traffic.

Intentionallies divided the main space into generously sized booths, where low walls topped by frosted glass provided seating for a maximum of two, giving clients a degree of privacy amid the hubbub. The frosted glass screens defining each booth were alternately green and white, imbuing each mini styling space with a dynamic contrast in colours as light filtered through from the neighbouring booths. Adding an element of theatricality to a client's arrival is the floor, which is raised up one step. Intentionallies installed the 15 cm elevation so the clients, as they step up into the booth, felt as though they were stepping onto a stage.

Intentionallies also focused on the comfort of the client, and brought in chairs similar to those designed for the azura Omotesando project, as the same clients owned both hair salon firms. The chairs were wide, with armrests and a supportive back pad to offer the maximum comfort to clients. Overhead, a swarm of pendant lamps suspended at random from the ceiling cast a flattering light on clients. Made of fine bone china, the lampshades were so thin they were almost translucent. A pattern drawn onto the outer surface of each resulted in the lamps giving off a warm, lantern-like light. The sides of the long narrow space were glazed, offering clients an extensive view over the surrounding low-rise residential buildings. After dark, the reflections of the salon's lights in the glazed façades added a further, dramatic note to the space. Presiding over the entryway was a large, tub-shaped ceiling lamp. Made of strings of glass beads, it was the prefect, installation-like welcome to greet clients as they entered the salon.

A Hair Salon That is a Home From Home

Intentionallies used armchair-like seats to ensure customers had a relaxing experience in the Blanco Casual hairdresser's in Nagoya.

A Hand-drawn Graphic That Gives an Office Space
Both Brand and Corporate Identity

A Retail Interior Inspired by Travel

For a retail store in Harajuku owned by a former musician, Intentionallies crafted an interior focusing on the concept of travel. The firm placed a large display table in the middle of the space, effectively creating an island in the heart of the store. Visual merchandizing displays in the form of shelving units were set against the walls. On entering the space, shoppers are encouraged by the layout to go on a journey, travelling from one themed display to the next, arriving at each new collection of products as though arriving at a new destination. A 50-inch flat screen monitor greets clients as they enter. Screening clips that link the merchandise to foreign settings, the TV is also highlights the contrast between the exotic atmosphere in the store and the local surroundings, thanks to the view provided by a large window that looks out over the city. For the central table, flooring and walls, Intentionallies selected steel, reclaimed teak and stone sourced from far-flung locations to underscore the travel focus. The client was pleased with the completed interior, as the brief had requested the space be imbued with the feeling inspired by travel.

Blackboard Paint on the Walls of an Office Lounge Creates an Ideas Space for Drawing and Writing

anatelíer Yokohama

Retail Interiors With a French Influence

A fashion brand with a French aesthetic, anatelíer is popular in Japan. The label commissioned Intentionallies to create a flagship, or *maison*, and nine other boutiques across Japan. Intentionallies set out to instil an atelier-like atmosphere in the store interiors, to represent both the brand and the clothing collections. As the label was neither ornamental nor ostentatious, but embraced a French approach to fashion, Intentionallies took elements from French antiques and interiors and installed subtle variations on them within the spaces. For example, the decorative entry archways are modernized interpretations of outlines inspired by French furniture. 'We didn't want anything too elaborate or obvious,' says Shuwa Tei. The firm also collaborated with illustrators who drew directly on the walls of the interiors, emphasizing the strong commitment to the creative process at the core of the brand.

anatelíer Machida

anateliér Umeda

anateliér Nanba

anateliér Shinjuku

anateliér Urawa

Using Natural Materials to Craft a Refined Atmosphere

The Strawberry Fields apparel line is a well-known brand in Japan. When a menswear collection was launched – the line was originally solely womenswear – Intentionallies was brought in to renovate a series of shops to celebrate the expansion. The client asked Intentionallies to reflect the fashion brand's high-end image in the new interiors. Intentionallies drew on a wide range of different techniques to craft furniture and fittings that were as select and as carefully finished as the clothing in the collection.

The first store to be renovated was located in the basement of the Shinjuku station complex. Stone was sourced from Java and Kalimantan, islands in Indonesia, for installation-like stone walls that were built in the space. Craftsmen in Indonesia worked on the stone before it was shipped to Japan, carving the

discrete etchings that can be particularly clearly seen on the wall featuring the Strawberry Fields logo. To the rear of the main shop floor, a large white screen used as a space divider was crafted from Corian. The dozens of holes were not just cut out of the block, each one was carefully hand carved. Corian was also used for an amusing display table with a counter top that had been split in half; the left half was set slightly higher, on elegant stainless steel frame, than the right hand side.

Scattering easy chairs through the store was a thoughtful gesture, offering the partners or friends of shoppers a seat to take a break or to offer an opinion on a garment. The chair featured a cantilevered seat supported only on its front legs. Wrapped onto the frame are strips of tan leather that had been hand finished by a specialist harness maker, a

technique had been inspired by a leather wrapped fountain pen. Even though the aluminium frame was completely covered, it too was also a finely finished technical part, as it had been manufactured using the die casting process. A T-shaped steel clothing rail was also wrapped in leather, but only partially, as the corners are exposed. The glimpses of the metal subtly showed off the fine finish of the metal. After the Shinjuku station store was completed, Intentionallies went on to renovate four additional stores in Yokohama, Tenjin, Ikebukuro and Tachikawa.

Communication / Collaboration

Intentionallies

Modern Spaces Featuring a Wealth of Materials and Finishes, From Sandstone Etchings to Solid Steel Counter Tops

Using a High-tech Paint for a White Interior

Intentionallies was asked by the owner of via bus stop to design a totally white store interior. An obvious disadvantage of a white space is that it tends to get dirty easily, an important consideration as anything less than snowy white would detract dramatically from the otherwise eye-popping effect of the concept. To craft an interior that was both white and workable, Intentionallies looked for a solution in new technologies. The firm selected a newly developed mark- and stain-resistant white paint. The firm used the fluorinated paint to create a luminous white space.

Solution / Standpoint

Shuwa Tei says, 'Many projects begin with a request from the client; we ask ourselves: what is the problem to be solved? First we consider the aim of the client, then we establish the target to be achieved, all the while sharing our thoughts with the client. We do not look for answers by merely looking at our past work and reusing old solutions: we always take a fresh look and search for the best answer. It is important to us to convey our unique style to the client. In this way, we feel that we can share our goals with our client.

It has always been our aim and practice to act spontaneously and be the source of original ideas. In one scheme, for Hanamiduki in 1999, we became entrepreneurs and established a restaurant that was to be the inspiration for the entire programme. We tried our hands at something quite new. We took on not just the design but also the responsibilities of management, learning about the service industry, including the provision of food and the areas for cooking and eating, while always looking at the design from the point of view of both workers and customers. In doing this we found a variety of fundamental concepts. There are times when we feel that it is important to change our standpoint. This is how our partnership with the consumer electronics brand, amadana, started in 2002. We recognized that it was important first to create a parent company that would establish the principles of the design. On the basis of this rationale, we established a consumer electronics joint venture with our partner. This encouraged us to create a viable system in which we could profit and also take part in decision making.'

An Installation Made Using CD Cases to Define the Firm's Identity

Following a meeting with record company Toy's Factory in Shibuya in December 1996, Intentionallies was commissioned to create a new interior design for the clients' offices. The challenge was to carry out the work with minimum interruption of the clients' business operations, and to complete the work within 12 days. Intentionallies responded to the short timeframe by filling the office with fixtures and building a focal point for the entrance. The installation was made of rows of hundreds of empty CD cases, placed as if they were on a horizontal shelf, but then stacked 15 rows high, creating a square. The installation was then backlit. With the Toy's Factory logo providing subtle signage, the installation reinforced the brand and corporate identity of the music producer. In the rest of the space, Intentionallies used large shelving fixtures as both storage and room dividers. Raised partitions on the linden wood desks created cubicles, giving employees a degree of privacy.

White Insertions for Meeting Rooms and Shelving

The second time Intentionallies was brought in to craft interiors for Toy's Factory, the architectural firm was given a longer timeframe to work with, so the interior design was more extensive and the furniture was custom-made. To give participants privacy when holding a meeting, Intentionallies walled off sections of a much larger room to create a series of small, soundproof meeting rooms. Attractive rectangles of light were integrated into the walls of the cube-like meeting rooms. Elsewhere, giving a large, open plan office a distinctive look, Intentionallies designed a freestanding shelving system that was integrated into the wall. The shelving curved out overhead, creating a tunnel-like fluidity to the design. To retain a sense of order, the shelves were fitted with drawers. Up-lights set atop the shelving element provided a soft glow that contrasted sharply with the strip lighting in the ceiling that ran parallel to the shelving. Clear CD boxes featured in the refit. They were used to create small lights placed on individual desks. A short row of 20 cases was bookended in wood; with a bulb set in the wood frame, the cases were transformed into small, portable lamps that were used in the reception area, and in meeting rooms. No fewer than 2,400 blank CD discs were stacked in the entrances of the fifth and eighth floors, where they formed tall, slim freestanding columns.

Dividing Space According to Function

Shaping a quiet working environment for the music firm's employees in an area with considerable through traffic, Intentionallies left enough floor space for a wide corridor, then enclosed the remaining area with a glazed wall. Integrated into the design were wooden louvers fitted to the glass panels to give employees additional privacy.

Wall Illustrations to Reinforce Brand Identity

The music industry in Japan has experienced a rapid evolution in recent years. When it became apparent that consumers were buying music in non-traditional ways, Toy's Factory asked itself what could be done in-house to keep in step with the developments in the music world. Intentionallies was tasked with the challenge of updating the firm's interiors. The commission was fitting, as Intentionallies had not only completed several interior renovations for Toy's Factory over the years – with the initial collaborations when the architectural firm was first founded being particularly welcome – but Intentionallies had also acted as creative consultant for Toy's Factory in select arenas.

The brief from the clients contained quite specific requests and directions. The first was that the two meeting rooms be made a lot less like an office and more akin to a gallery, to provide Toy's Factory with suitable spaces for meetings with artists. The walls of the larger area were to be illustrated and the names of particular artists the firm had in mind were passed to Intentionallies. A number of the artists were creatives whose music had been produced by the Toy's Factory label. Abstract yet powerful, the illustrations applied directly onto the wall in the larger space are by Kenjirou Harigai of Adapter and BELX3 & ESOW. As the clients were keen that the illustrated space had the atmosphere of a gallery, furniture in those areas had slim, simple forms so as to not distract attention from the expressive artwork. All the furniture was also freestanding to give the clients the flexibility, when needed, to move or rearrange the chairs and tables, depending on the event staged.

Some of the artists asked Intentionallies if they could do more than draw on the walls. A glass panel stretching the width of the meeting room has been etched by Tycoon Graphics, who delivered the graphic data to Intentionallies for the firm to execute the work. With the addition of a chandelier by Madeine Boulesteix, the work of these artists was integrated into the three-dimensional nature of the space. Adding to the lounge-like atmosphere in the meeting room were glossy panels featuring photography of giant flowers on a black background, the work of Hiro Sugiyama of Enlightenment. A comfortable sofa that runs the length of the room, and stools, are all finished in chocolate-coloured leather and have a pared down profile to avoid creating a contrast with the installations. Elsewhere is a rather more elaborate sofa by Masamichi Katayama, of Wonderwall.

To deliver what the clients wished, Intentionallies used a very small selection of materials, but the firm deployed stainless steel, glass and leather, creating a subtle backdrop to the artists' installations which stand as a powerful reference to the creativity that drives the firm.

A Vinyl Store With a Gallery-like Interior

'At one stage, flicking through vinyl records was all I did for a while,' says Shuwa Tei. 'I focused on each record as I flipped through a pile and I felt at one with the world,' he adds. The store Tei frequented most was Dance Music Record in Shibuya, so when the owner of the shop approached Intentionallies in 1999 for a refit, Tei was delighted to work on a space he had been so attached to.

The client requested an interior that was bright and organized, rather than dark and dingy which typified music stores at the time. Intentionallies opened up the two-storey space, creating well-lit interiors with white walls and ceilings. The firm made the most of the record cover artwork by designing display shelving in linden wood with a tannin oil finish that gave the jackets maximum exposure, creating a gallery-like effect. Also in light-coloured wood were the listening stations, which were the very latest technology at the time of the store's reopening, when Intentionallies' innovative approach to the record store interior shook up the competition right across the district.

The shop was still trading early in 2010. Although music appreciation is evolving all the time, vinyl enthusiasts can but hope that the rare find that is Dance Music Record remains a Tokyo fixture.

Shaping an Atmosphere Using Light and Shadows

Nightclubs are often very dark, so when Intentionallies was commissioned to shape the interior for Apollo, a club in Aoyama, the firm set out to address the lighting aspect. A club, in essence, is lighting and music, with guests adding to the atmosphere generated by the space itself. Intentionallies used lighting and reflections to set the right mood, focusing also on shadows to ensure the space didn't become too bright. The principal installations were a series of reflective panels. Each screen was made of several rows of small, stainless steel rectangles threaded into columns and then assembled in rows to form a large panel. Shifting slightly in gusts of air as clubbers walked by, the panels reflected light from nearby mirror balls and spotlights, sending circles of light to play over the walls behind the DJ booth and across the ceiling of the lounge.

Intentionallies | Solution / Standpoint

Using Light and Reflection to Craft an Interior

Strict building regulations in Tokyo resulted in the brief for a nightspot that Intentionallies had been commissioned to renovate being changed. In addition, during the planning permission approval process, the client opted for a different design direction, so what had originally been a restaurant, bar and club became a lounge bar.

The concept for Lounge O that got the eventual go-ahead was for a space with an atmosphere that was informed by Intentionallies' selection of materials and custom-designed furniture. The first obstacle the firm had to overcome was to prevent a pair of enormous structural columns from dominating the space. Intentionallies' solution was to hide the columns. The firm flanked each column in mirrors that reflect to infinity the strings of Swarovski crystals and beads suspended alongside. More than merely minimizing the presence of the columns, the use of mirrors creates the impression that the

columns have completely disappeared and have been replaced by a three-dimensional shape. Thanks to the myriad reflections, each cube-like volume looks as if it has been filled with an elegant, jewelled forest.

Intentionallies contrasted the high-tech columns with more traditional techniques. Rear walls are flanked in sandstone sourced in Java where skilled artisans carved a modern, geometric pattern into the surface. Spotlights directed at the wall highlight the dry texture of the stone, creating a graphic backdrop. Grouped around slim Corian tables are sleek sofas covered in suede and juxtaposed alongside are low stools hewn from solid pieces of wood. Although sanded smooth, the wood has not been treated, giving it a raw, natural feel. Overhead, ceiling lamps were made using a technique known as *bunaco*, where craftsmen coiled strips of beech and then shaped the coils into wide, shallow, dish-like lampshades.

Using cooking as a simile to refer to the many raw ingredients that, when combined in the right proportion, produce an exquisite result, Shuwa Tei explains, 'The number and combination of materials used strike the right balance. It's like we selected ingredients that were totally different from normal and used them to shape a new recipe.'

foundation of rhythmic movement
prime sound studio

A Soundscape
for a Recording Studio

The music studio Prime Sound Studio FORM
(Foundation of Rhythmic Movement) is located in
Shibuya. When Intentionallies renovated the interior of
the studio's basement space, the focus was on the
sound-related, functional requirements needed for each
room. The size and structure of each space Intentionallies designed was determined by the acoustical specifications the client requested for each environment.
Smaller recording studios were used for individual instru-
ments or voices, and larger spaces were necessary for
big groups of artists.

Intentionallies | Solution / Standpoint

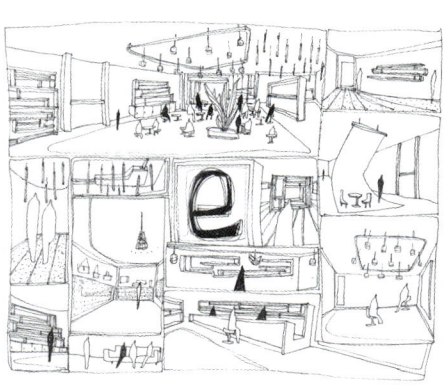

A Landscape Informed by Fixtures

Ecru Sannomiya

Intentionallies was brought in to design the interior for lifestyle store Ecru in the Sannomiya district of Tokyo. Intentionallies' concept was to configure the space by taking everyday objects that shoppers would be familiar with and using them in an unexpected way. Fluorescent strip lighting was mounted horizontally, rather than vertically, giving the basic tube lamps a fresh appeal. Display fixtures were built from chipboard, a material commonly used as a structural element, but rarely seen as a surface material. The rough textures and basic materials gave the space an honest feel.

Ecru Venus Fort

The second store Intentionallies completed for Ecru was located in the large shopping mall complex in Tokyo called Venus Fort. The concept the firm presented the client with was the creation of a landscape within a landscape. Intentionallies build a number of stainless steel fixtures. The long ends of several counter tops lifted up in the air like a wave. One display looked as though individual shelves had shifted right or left, creating a strong sense of originality in the store. Elsewhere, strips of stainless steel set into the floor merged seamlessly with the walls, adding further interest to the store design.

A Warehouse-like Space to Display Interior Furnishings

Dailies is a lifestyle shop located in Mitaka, Tokyo. Intentionallies was brought in to give it a restyle. One of the most important factors in the renovation was the planning and organization of the project, as half the shop remained open for business during construction. In addition, the timeframe was very tight, with less than two months allocated for the whole refit, from concept through construction to completion.

Intentionallies set out to strip the store back to its skeleton. The firm didn't replace the ceiling, but left the air ducts exposed overhead, giving the store an industrial aesthetic. While the focus was on leaving as much of the space as unfinished as possible, the floor, however, was finished. It was laid with wood, to present the interior furnishings in a homely environment. Dainty pendant lamps suspended on long wires provided an ironic contrast to the raw, construction-like nature of the bare ceiling.

Solution / Standpoint

Intentionallies

An Entrance Atrium Featuring Lines
of Light That Guide Customers to the Department Store

The White Background and Furniture in a Camera and Printing Store Focus Customers' Attention on the Colour-coded Products

A Journey Round the World via Interiors

When Intentionallies was asked to renovate the interiors of several stores for eyewear specialist JIN's, the architectural firm worked with the client to create individual concepts for each store in the eyewear chain. The glasses in the collection are produced in Korea, so when Intentionallies started work on the first store to be refitted, which was located in Kichijoji, the firm drew on elements from Korean history. Marketing the high-quality, affordable glasses required a strong interior, so Intentionallies ensured the entry – which faced the road – was eye-catching. Setting the store apart from its neighbours is an elegant door frame made of latticed wood. Adjacent buildings are either historic, and have been renovated, or modern, so the statement-making entrance struck a balance between the contrasting styles in the surrounding cityscape. Inside are antiques dating from Korea's Joseon dynasty, simultaneously inspiring the Japanese clients with the reference to this historic period, and reminding them of the exotic country where the products were created.

The remainder of the shops were located in big shopping malls, so Intentionallies felt that ensuring each JIN's store stood out from its neighbours was vital, so this became the focus, rather than imbuing the store with the context of a given location. Intentionallies ensured, nonetheless, that each store had its own theme, however subtle, that was connected with travelling around the world, while still maintaining a strong brand identity.

The second shop the firm renovated was in Kamoi, a suburb of Yokohama. Intentionallies had to begin designing the concept for the store before the neighbouring shops had been fitted up, so the firm had no idea what the interiors installed on either side would be like. The firm opted for an Indonesian, and in particular, a Balinese atmosphere. Hand-carved sandstone and dark walnut fixtures with brass handles set against a white background emphasized the dignity and strength of the materials, while the warm indirect lighting added to the ambiance, setting the elegant eyewear displays off against a contrasting backdrop.

JIN's Kichijoji

JIN's Maebashi

JIN's Yokohama

JIN's Hanyu

JIN's Kagamihara

JIN's Senshu

JIN's Koshigaya

JIN's Niigata

JIN's Morioka

A Presentation That Can Be Reassembled Quickly

Affordable fashion has become the goal of the apparel industry, so when asked to craft interiors for the stores of fashion label YEVS, Intentionallies came up with an architectural version of the concept: a carefully constructed space that had a sense of tension and expressed consistency but had the flexibility to allow for change.

In the store design, columns positioned at regular intervals created a visual tension, and by scaling the fitting rooms to reflect the dimensions of the columns, Intentionallies minimized the number of elements installed in the interior, ensuring it remained functional. The fashion collection is presented on a series of parallel bars that form a very structured set of clothing rails. Set slightly out from the walls, the display system offered considerable flexibility. In the same way that a garment can give a very different impression according to how it is worn, the display system can be rearranged to suit different shaped items of clothing. It was designed to enable a speedy reorganization of the displays in order to present new collections as soon as they arrived, fitting neatly into the brand's concept of 'fast fashion'.

Made from steel painted a matt black, the floor-to-ceiling bars in the systematic display system not only provide railings to present clothing, but are also used to frame the mirrors that reach the full height of the interior. Used also in the window display, the graphic system becomes a bold decorative element.

United Arrows Ikebukuro

Store Aesthetics That Blend Japanese and Western Influences

United Arrows stocks hip clothing handpicked from around the globe, as well as producing its own collections. For the renovation of the United Arrows store in Ikebukuro, Intentionallies took inspiration from aspects of Japanese culture adding some western influences, to mirror the source of the clothing collections sold in store. The architectural firm installed a glass tunnel in the entryway, with water splashing down onto the glass. Protected by the glazing overhead, shoppers – as they walk through the tunnel – are treated to a display of pretty reflections on the walls, created by the interplay of light and water. In the store, some areas are open and are well lit. In contrast, a passageway leading to the fitting rooms is very narrow, evoking a Japanese-like path found in a city such as Kyoto. In the passageway, slim bamboo poles flank one side of corridor, which is softly lit by pebble lamps made, according to tradition, from paper.

United Arrows Nagoya

Using Sculptural Installations as Display Systems

The entrance of the United Arrows shop that Intentionallies renovated in Nagoya faces the south side of a busy shopping street. Given the long, slim configuration of the shop, the architectural firm used lighting as near natural as possible. The concept of melding Japanese and western styles was extended to this store too, where stained glass, a western technique, was installed above the entrance, but finished in a Japanese pattern and colour scheme, which included gold hues. Inside the store, the displays are sculptural. A glass stairway climbs up towards the ceiling. It leads nowhere, instead forming a most eye-catching display system.

United Arrows Shibuya

An Unexpected Place for a Garden

Intentionallies designed the façade and fitting rooms for the United Arrows shop in Shibuya. The walls of the ground and first floor that front the street are glazed, transparent on the lower floor and translucent on the upper level. The glass boxes installed in the façade reappear in miniature as the changing rooms, where a surprise lies in store for shoppers: grass is laid between each cubicle and to the rear of each compartment. The bright green of the real grass growing indoors forms an astonishingly strong contrast to the surrounding interior. The gardens are tiny, but they nonetheless make shoppers smile in unexpected delight.

It was a stroke of good fortune that, some years back, I happened to share a taxi with Tyler Brûlé when we were on the same design awards jury. I was getting ready to make a research trip to Tokyo and, since Tyler always has a finger on the design pulse, I asked him what I should see and who I should meet. At least three of his recommendations are still on my Tokyo top ten list today: Hakusan, Wonderwall and Shuwa Tei.

Not long after I arrived in Tokyo, Tei and his colleagues at Intentionallies invited me over to see more of their work. Since most studio visits are of the 'show and tell' variety, I was honoured that their invitation also included dinner, prepared and served in their space. In one extremely pleasant evening I was treated to the complete Intentionallies experience: we met in a beautiful space they designed; the elegant dinner – fresh, simple, and seasonal – was presented as Tei would have presented a meal at his Hanamiduki restaurant; and we discussed their work in a convivial, social setting. This one evening was important to my understanding of how the various pieces of the Intentionallies portfolio fit together.

Unlike many North American practices, which are too often limited to a single area of design, Intentionallies works across a broad design spectrum that includes everything from calculators to skyscrapers. Like a well-crafted music playlist, interior design, product design and architecture mix together seamlessly in the firm's creative practice. The amadana shops in Nakameguro (BALS STORE) and Omotesando Hills are a brilliant example of this *gesamtkunstwerk* approach. Tei believes that a well-designed product can be placed anywhere and, by virtue of its design, can change the scenery around it. Most of us are so used to buying off-the-shelf appliances that we think more about their functionality and, let's face it, their price than their design. Who would think of a microwave oven as a beautiful object? Shuwa Tei and his colleagues think just that. The amadana microwave with its sleek shape and natural wood handle brings pleasure to even a minute-long defrosting job and deserves to be shown off right next to the most beautiful serving dish in the house. I often recommend that design lovers include one of the amadana shops on their Tokyo sightseeing itineraries. Why would we want to visit an appliance store, they inevitably ask. Because, I explain, amadana is not an appliance store. It's a museum, a curio shop, a showroom where all the oft-overlooked accoutrements of our daily lives – juicers, calculators, microwaves, televisions – are presented with style, dignity, and the same reverence with which one would exhibit sculpture in a gallery. This is what design is all about: the quiet beauty of the everyday.

The spirit and conceptual thinking behind Intentionallies' work is really only one-half of the equation. The other half is the heart of the work that Tei and his partners make: products we want to use and display, interiors we want to spend time in, buildings we want to point out to our friends and, if we're really lucky, live in for a lifetime. The desire for permanence, dependability, and endurance is not new to architecture but in Tei's case it springs not from ego but from respect. His statement that he would like to make products that people can take care of sounds strange to North American ears. This is what we say about our children, our grandparents, and our pets. Not about our staplers and tape dispensers. But it is this deep and profound humanity that makes the work of Intentionallies so timeless, especially in today's throwaway society when much of contemporary design has more to do with glamour and gimmickry than with problem-solving and good old-fashioned usefulness.

Tei balances his love of mid-century design – think of Wegner's Scandinavian simplicity or the experimental California spirit of the Eameses – with a rigor and a subtractive approach to design on the one hand and an unerring attention to detail and an abiding affection for materials on the other. At times, the work of Intentionallies can seem severe – curves are nowhere to found and forms are pared down to their barest essence – but, yet, the results are not cold and antiseptic. Every Intentionallies product and interior melds the contemporary with the classic by combining the natural tactility of leather and wood with the industrial strength and sleekness of plastic, glass, aluminium, and stainless steel to give products, interiors, and buildings alike a strong sense of warmth and dignity. And, every so often, a pop of pure colour makes us smile.

Perhaps it should go without saying that there is a definite Japaneseness to the work of Intentionallies. Respect for tradition and a sense of quiet beauty exist side-by-side with innovation and originality. Intentionallies works with time-honoured materials and the latest technology to create products and places that mesh perfectly with our fast-paced lifestyles yet make us want to slow down and appreciate their beauty. And take care of them. Maybe even forever.

Brooke Hodge
Director, Exhibition Management and Publications, Hammer Museum, Los Angeles

The Evolution of Design Fashioned by Time

Shuwa Tei begins, 'I have been thinking about the relationship between Tokyo and the rest of the world from the Japanese angle. They say that the apparent distance between Japan and the rest of Asia, and between the East and the West is shrinking but I feel that it is inevitable that Japan's designs are being distilled from its original culture and crystallized with the passage of time. I would like to be able to understand creative inspiration but this cannot be achieved merely by collecting facts. In places where temporal and spatial axes cross like the warp and weft of fabric, I want to create original but inevitable solutions that are the two-way marriage of the interior with the exterior. To continue my acquisition of information I search out different places, finding new opportunities and occasionally creating new forms.'

A Cultural Remix Hotel

'Our treatment of Hotel Claska epitomizes our general approach,' says Shuwa Tei, 'Because the project initiated a reflection, which in this case focused on how best to live.'

Meguro, the road where Claska is located, is in an up-and-coming Tokyo district with many interior design and lifestyle stores attracting young, affluent Tokyoites to the neighbourhood. The building Claska occupies was constructed over 35 years ago. Until 2002, it functioned as a business hotel. When that folded, reviving the site as a hotel was considered extremely problematic because a hotel-only venue was no longer deemed a viable option, given the way the surrounding area was developing. Intentionallies had originally been asked to install a new hotel and lounge in the existing building. However, during the initial discussions with the client, it became apparent that a programme comprising a greater mix of activities would be more successful. The shift led to Intentionallies investigating how guests spend their time in hotels and what they really want from a visit. Together with the client, Intentionallies then came up with an innovative solution. Claska was freed from the framework of operating only as a hotel and reincarnated as a hotel that was also a cultural destination, with a gallery, lounge, bar, restaurant and more, to appeal to the hip design enthusiasts flocking to the area.

'To us, renovation means considering all aspects of the design while being faithful to the original concept and changing the function of an old building while at the same time beautifying it,' says Shuwa Tei. Before Intentionallies could begin the process of renovating the building however, the business model had to be rewritten, to establish how the investment required could be met by the limited funds available. The shortfall 'was the clue', says Tei, as it stimulated the firm into finding a daring way to move forward. Intentionallies narrowed its focus to just nine guest rooms, which were divided between the fourth and fifth floors, and the ground floor lounge with its restaurant, bar and DJ booth. As soon as the renovation of these spaces was complete, they were opened. The income generated provided the necessary financing to refurbish the remaining floors in the eight-storey building. 'This strategy allowed us

to reduce the initial outlay,' says Tei simply. Instead of going on to add additional hotel rooms, the project was completed with 30 residential units for longer-term stays, and a gallery, dog-grooming salon, bookstore and gift shop, establishing Claska's wide-reaching appeal.

With a façade – designed by London-based creative agency Tomato – consisting of three-dimensional, fibre-reinforced plastic and an interactive light installation in its entryway, Claska offers visitors a strongly contemporary first encounter, whether they are dropping by to meet friends at the bar, or heading to the dog-grooming salon with their pet. The concept of a building offering accommodation that also has an active hub attracting non-residents, while common in Europe and the United States, was almost unheard of in Japan. When it opened, Claska was heralded as one of Tokyo's first boutique hotels.

Tokyo is not only the capital of Japan but it is also one of Asia's most important cities. Due to its geographical location however, it is not a transit city like Hong Kong or Bangkok. To this end, Intentionallies was eager that Claska should exude an authentic Japanese atmosphere, anchoring the building in its location. Tei explains, 'Claska was to welcome guests from around the world so it was important for us to use traditional Japanese techniques and materials, to establish a strong sense of place.'

Many architects working during the 20th century not only created architectural masterpieces but they also designed the furniture and fittings to go in them. Frank Lloyd Wright, in particular, believed that interior elements were integral to the overall design, and completed his buildings with custom-made furniture and fittings. Likewise, Intentionallies designed much of the furnishings and lighting for Hotel Claska.

In contrast to the vibrant exterior and entrance, the reception area exudes a tranquil atmosphere and is furnished with elements that draw on Japanese traditions. Tubular lamps placed on the reception desk and suspended overhead were made in brass and have a

brushed finish, achieved using a potter's wheel. Creating the metalwork forms presented the team of artisans with a challenge as the techniques and tools used are more typically seen in the making of alter fittings for Buddhist temples. Needless to say, Intentionallies was pleased with the result. The reception desk was also custom treated. Used on its own, lacquer paint has a gloss finish, so hemp was added to the lacquer applied to the reception desk panels, giving a richer, more textured finish.

In the lounge, drum-shaped ceiling lamps made of tin were textured using hammers. Shades for floor lamps were made using a technique known as *bunako* , where craftsmen coil strips of beech and then shape the coils into the desired form. Much of the custom-designed furniture was crafted from Japanese mahogany. The fact that it is favoured by carpenters who find it easier to carve than other hardwoods is illustrated in a series of benches featuring *shippou*, an intricate, traditional Japanese pattern, which has been cut out of the back panels. In another nod to the past, antique tea sets, which would have been used in tea ceremonies, are table centrepieces. Tei explains, 'Creating the right atmosphere was a priority.'

Elsewhere, the firm's attention to detail encompasses wooden flooring flanking the terrace which features a subtle *Naguri* wave, a traditional Kyoto treatment, but in a novel twist, it has been laid in a herringbone configuration. 'We are passionate about details,' says Tei, 'Even if they are so subtle that guests may scarcely notice, they add balance and harmony throughout.'

While a number of young creatives have moved in to the customizable residential units, others have chosen to site their office at Claska, attracting a vibrant crowd of friends and colleagues whose presence at the bar and restaurant add to Claska's allure. Tei concludes, 'One of the reasons why architecture can be considered a comprehensive art form is because the totality of social life and living can be integrated within the volume of a structure. In other words, architecture breathes new life into the structure that it creates.'

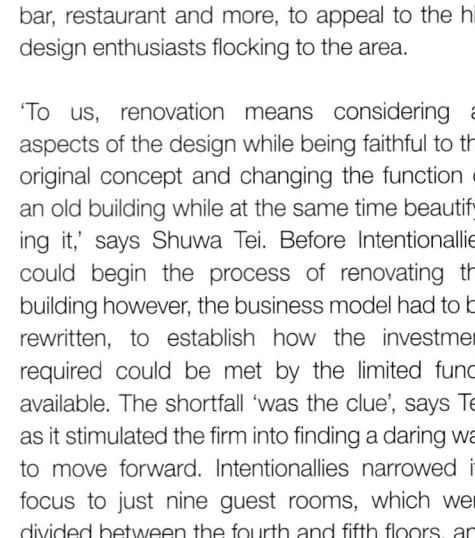

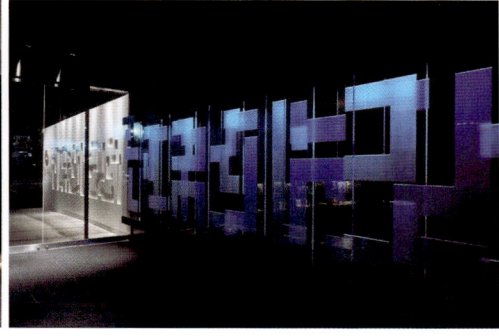

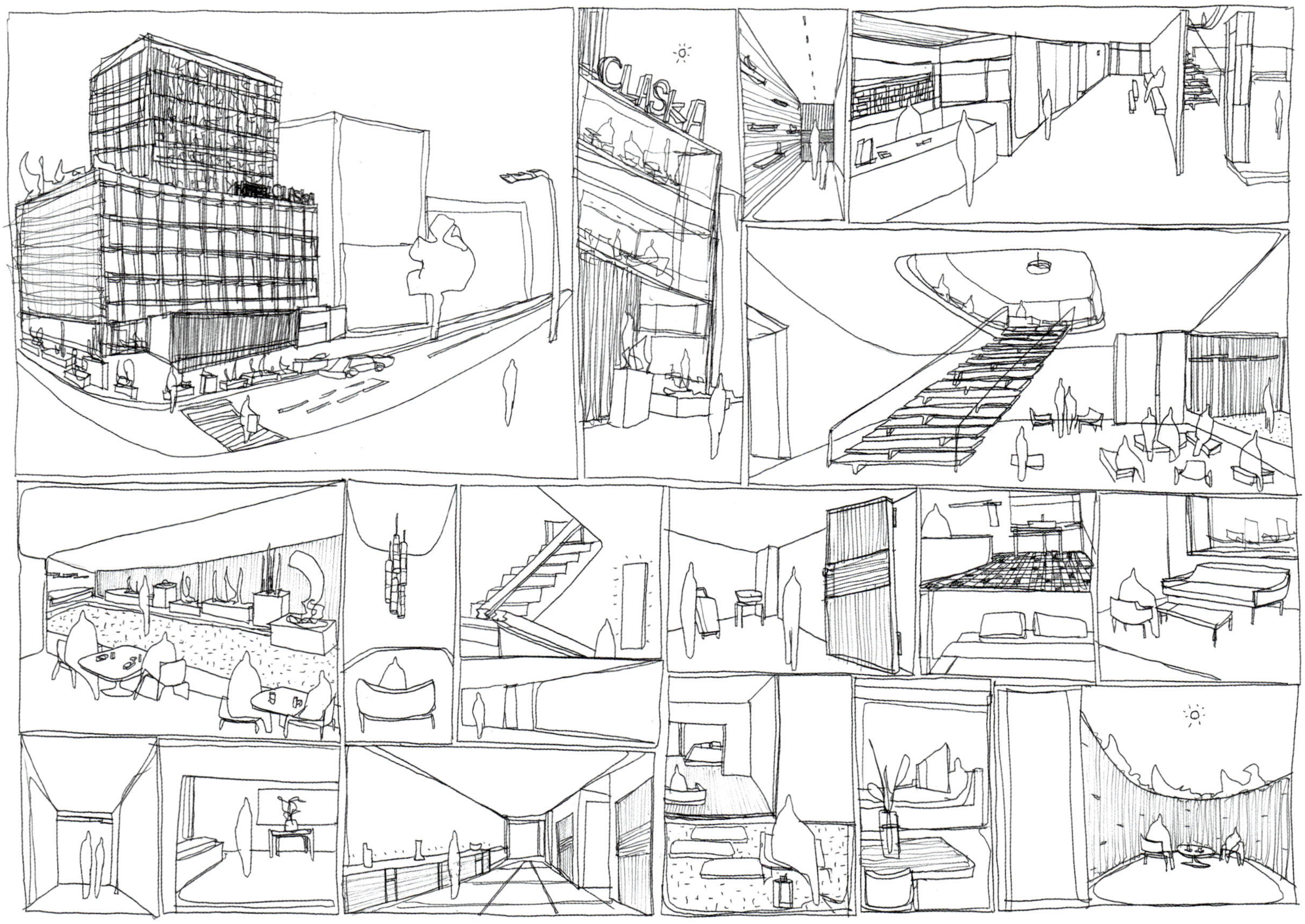

Proof of beauty
and its appearance

'It's our mission to create a piece of work that embodies what Intentionallies is about at a certain point in time,' says Shuwa Tei. As the firm was celebrating its 10th anniversary, Intentionallies started working on a private venture in Tokyo's Jingumae district, having just completed Hanamiduki (see page 084-087) in the same area. The lower half of the new-build project – from basement to the third floor – was to be the new office for Intentionallies, and the upper half, a private residence. The plans had been conceived four years prior to the acquisition of the land. But construction had to be postponed for a further year due the costs, which had ballooned beyond original estimates. The increase occurred mainly because the plans had to be revised due to local construction laws, which didn't permit a building of the height that Intentionallies had originally planned. The firm had to 'find a solution that was most relevant to our approach at the time', explains Tei.

The volume of the six-storey building was informed by its trapezium-shaped plot, a feature that many buildings located in Tokyo share. 'Above all, we were interested in giving the residence a daring presence, as if to defy the default building type in the Jingumae area which is white, light and appearing to float,' elaborates Tei. The cedar frame of the building is exposed in the exterior concrete walls. Intentionallies brought out the natural ring pattern in the surface of the wood by polishing the exposed timbers. The roof, meanwhile, is a deep green natural slate. Cut unevenly, it has an organic texture. 'The contrasting relationship of these materials describes the architecture perfectly,' says Tei.

What makes an architectural project an Intentionallies' building is, Tei explains, 'A question we have often eagerly asked ourselves. Ultimately, we decided that it is when the total ensemble is in perfect harmony.' Rather than remodelling the original architectural form, Intentionallies worked hard to bring out the characteristics of each floor, and in doing so, the studio made full use of various materials and techniques. The shutters in the residential modules are crafted from well-seasoned rosewood that had been carefully hand picked and then polished in Bali, after being harvested from Java.

While the trace of each material was perfectly blended, the firm ensured that the project did not turn into an exhibition of materials. Tei explains that, 'By constantly bouncing lines and planes off of each other, we believe that we have successfully achieved a high-level formula to unify different materials. By playing with lines instead of focusing on techniques, we have drawn them as if preparing a dinner where each course is a harmonious part of the whole, in addition to each dish being delicious and distinctive.'

The uniformity and harmony of the architecture was achieved by the firm being hands-on and adding its own perspectives to the interior and exterior design and the furnishings, instead of simply handing over the design drawings to a construction company. Tei concludes, 'We hope visitors to the building sense the harmony we established, a harmony that will not loose its lustre with the passing of time.'

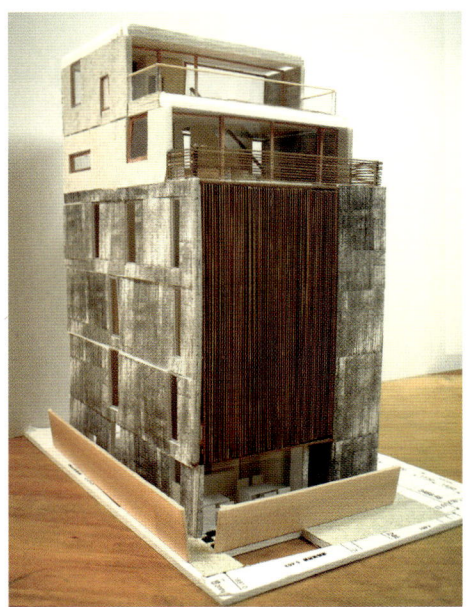

Intentionallies   The Evolution of Design Fashioned by Time

A Space for Both Living and Working

A residential block with integrated work spaces, Holland Hills is a project that illustrates Intentionallies' endeavour to move away from a single purpose space and create an area where offices and residences can coexist. Following discussions with the client, the firm focused on four specific target groups, honing the work environments to the occupants' professional require-ments. For example, photographic studios were built in a number of the units because photographers were one of the occupations selected. In addition, Intentionallies felt that certain social needs of the residents had to be addressed, whether that was providing space for hobbies or home entertaining, which layout alone would not resolve. Taking hardware to be the furniture and fittings, and software to be the lifestyle of an individual, Shuwa Tei explains, saying, 'It's not enough to provide for the hardware aspect, you also have to focus on the software.'

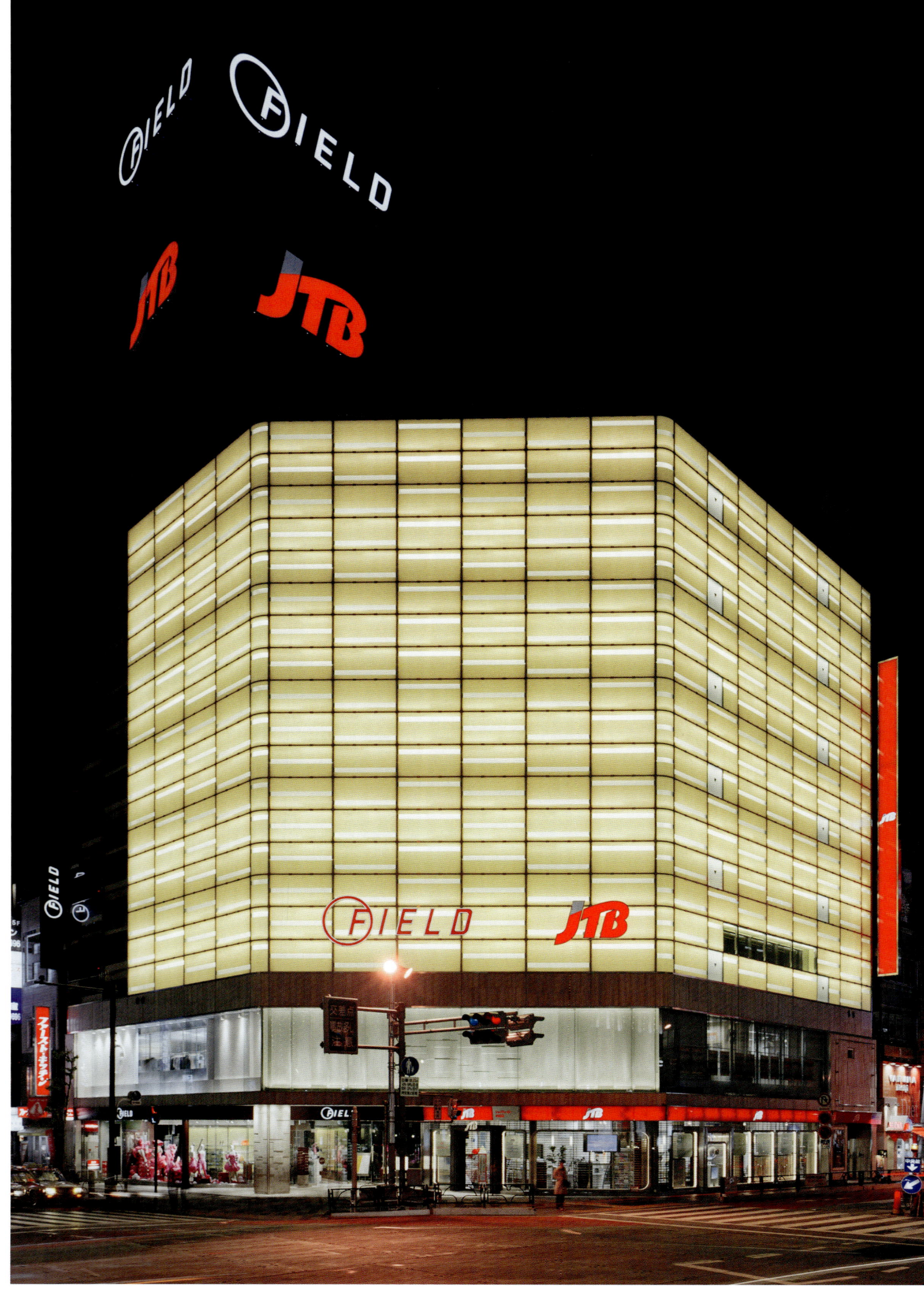

A Monumental Façade That Lights up Its Surroundings

A department store located on Shinjuku's biggest intersection had such a prominent site that although Intentionallies was initially commissioned to complete the interior, the firm put forward a concept for the façade too. 'The location,' explains Shuwa Tei, 'Called for an iconic landmark.' The client was so impressed by Intentionallies' mono-lithic design for Marui Field that the firm was given the go-ahead for the exterior.

Intentionallies set out to create a beacon, but as Shinjuku already has a superabundance of neon signs, it was decided that the store's façade should not feature neon or LEDs. Instead, the firm opted for a Japanese lantern-like concept. Both the profile and the materials used have echoes of a lantern, transforming the façade into an enormous, softly glowing lighting element that stands out from its flashy surroundings.

Rising eight storeys high, the building can be seen from each approach to the massive junction. While the façade was obviously not made of paper and thin strips of wood like an actual lantern, it was crafted from a carefully chosen set of materials that created an effect very similar to one. Intentionallies used a wood skin lamination, a new material developed for the automotive industry, where it is referred to as a high-performing decorated film. Wood has certain properties which make it unsuitable for many exterior applications, so Aura, the Kyoto-based firm of specialists who developed the material, ensured that it was durable by coating the film no fewer than five times, enabling it to withstand harsh environments. The glass used across the façade was laminated with the film, the different hues designed to enhance the lantern-like effect. The entire façade was then backlit.

This multi-functional film is made of special resin, strengthened by cross-linking by exposure to an electron beam, making it potentially very useful in design. Intentionallies has tried to standardize this technology for the first time in the field of architecture, in co-operation with Aura.

Department stores usually have a single theme uniting all the floors, so the whole store looks very much the same. However, in the interior for Marui Field, Intentionallies gave each floor its own theme. Some are abstract, but the floor selling sportswear, for example, has a tropical context, to tie in with its swimwear collections. The lifts provide the connection that links the floors.

The first floor gives the impression of being out of doors. The concept is enhanced by the studio and the cafe being placed in what appears to be a field, with images of sporting activities scattered on the ground. The casual air of the sports floor gradually gives way to the more dignified tone of the next floor up. The entry to each floor forms a dramatic encounter for the customer, a key factor in sales promotion. Customers can appreciate the experience of shopping at the store by imagining that they are playing sports there.

Creating a Roomscape

AGITO, a high-end lifestyle store in Tokyo's Roppongi Hills, stocks furniture and interior accessories. The shop occupies 1,500 m² and is spread over two floors. Intentionallies' concept for the space was the creation of a roomscape. As the shop sold items sourced both worldwide and from within Japan, Intentionallies integrated western and oriental styles. Greeting clients as they approach the shop is a pair of enormous doors. Stretching from floor to ceiling, the doors are made of panels arranged in a herringbone format, which is unusual as it more normally seen in flooring. In contrast to the European pattern is the subtle Japanese *naguri* wave, a traditional Kyoto treatment, carved into the surface of the wood. On the upper level of the store, the teak floor is laid according to a traditional Korean design, *chosen-bari*. Juxtaposing the floor with the modern glazed walls of the shop made a rich contrast. Intentionallies' focus on detail was extended to the decoration of the vents covering the air conditioning, which was inspired by technique of cloisonné. Intentionallies' focus on detail was extended to the decoration of the vents covering the air conditioning. The decorative pattern carved into covers features Japanese symbols called *shippo*, the Japanese term for cloisonné, and appears almost as if it had been carved into the actual wall. Spanning Japanese, oriental and western concepts, the design for AGITO places the products displayed neatly in context.

Intentionallies   The Evolution of Design Fashioned by Time

A Cinema Complex

A cinema complex can be considered as a collective entity of an established system because every element, from the layout and the flow of pedestrian traffic to the concession stand menu, serves the primary function of providing entertainment.

Intentionallies developed the concept for United Cinema Toyosu, a 12-screen multiplex in the south of Tokyo, by challenging the design scheme used for cinemas at that time, when multiple screen complexes were not common in Japan. In addition, the firm was briefed to take full advantage of the ocean front location and create a cinema that borrowed from the surrounding scenery to encourage audiences to linger after the film screening. Key to the success of the project was overcoming negative stereotypes like neon signs and popcorn.

As the cinema had recently been sold to a Japanese company by the foreign firm that had owned it, a change of logo was also required. Intentionallies developed a new logo based on a grid, suspending lettering within a metal framework. The firm crowned the foyer with the resulting bold graphic, and then used it as the template to provide signage throughout.

Each area in the complex has distinctive characteristics. The white-based hues in the foyer provide a welcoming, serene environment. As the cinema-goers progress through the zones en route to the film they've come to see, a sense of anticipation is generated through the rich palette of colours used in the concessions counter area. The feeling of expectation is then heightened because, in order to move from the ticketing zone towards the screens, the cinema-goers must pass ritual-like under an indoor waterfall, evoking a dramatic scene in a film.

The walls extending from the entry zone into the centre of the complex are flanked in Pallas stone finished by Bali artisans. Etched into the stone are engravings, based on he client's new company logo, designed by Intentionallies. Elsewhere, texture was applied to walls and columns, enhancing the neutral hues, which are offset by the dynamic carpet pattern in the corridors connecting the auditoriums.

Offering respite from the crowds and the noise is the Silent Lounge, one of the largest of the chill-out spaces, where a glazed wall provides a calming view across Tokyo Bay. To counter the common perception of toilets being a negative space, Intentionallies also replaced an exterior wall with floor-to-ceiling glazing in the bathrooms, filing the washbasin area with natural light during the day.

As Shuwa Tei explains, 'Each space become a stage where the boundary between reality and fiction becomes blurred, presenting people with the illusion that they have wandered into a film set.' The final installation uniting the decorative scheme is revealed in the exclusive private lounge on the second floor. On a black satin lacquerware wall, the cinema's logo is depicted in Swaroski crystals. 'The diverse components form a cohesive whole,' says Tei, continuing, 'We are confident that the sequence of sets that the cinema-goer progresses through, which has not been seen before outside Japan, could become an international standard for future cinema complexes.'

SCREEN ← TICKETS

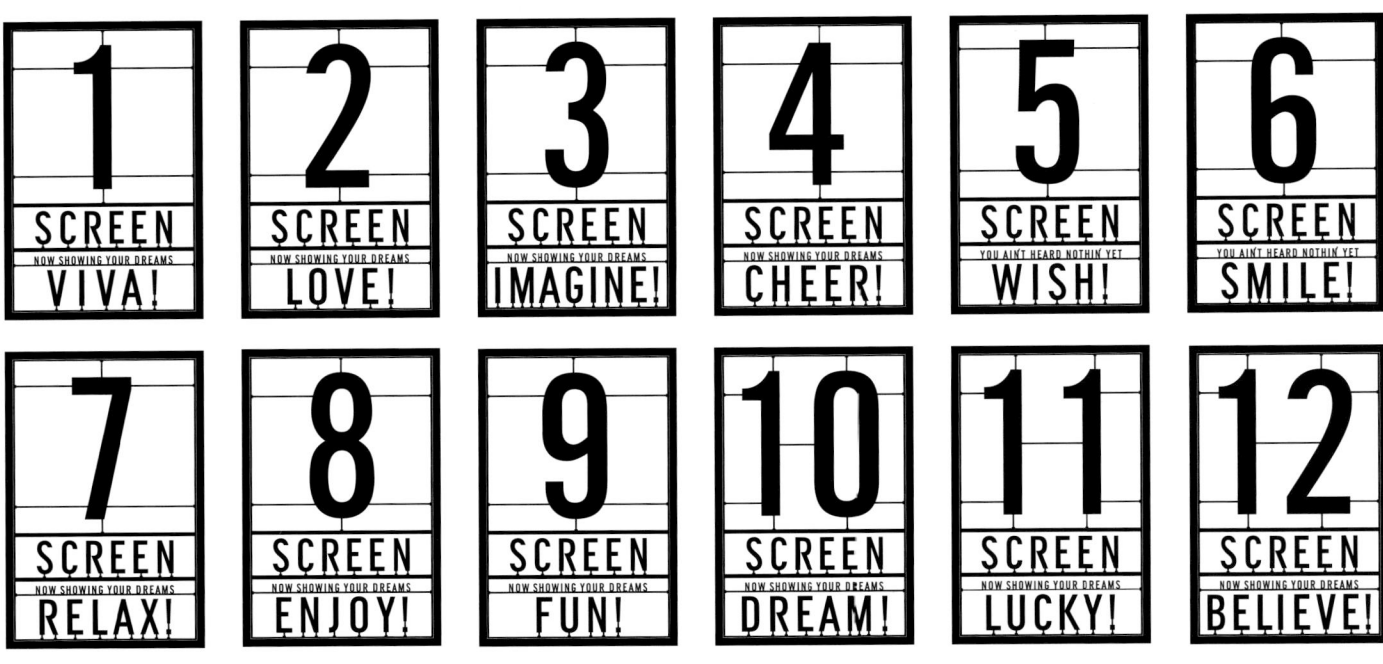

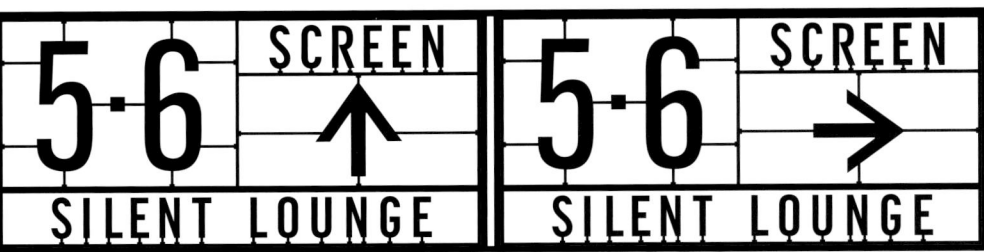

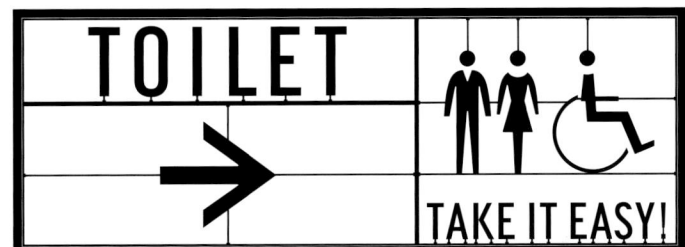

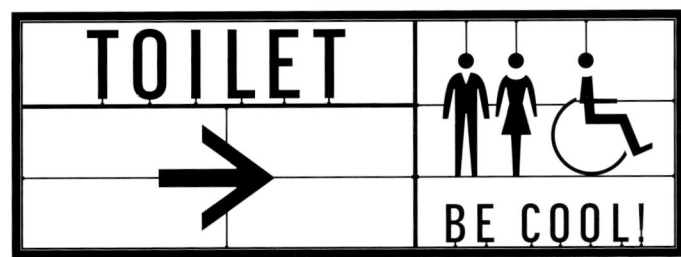

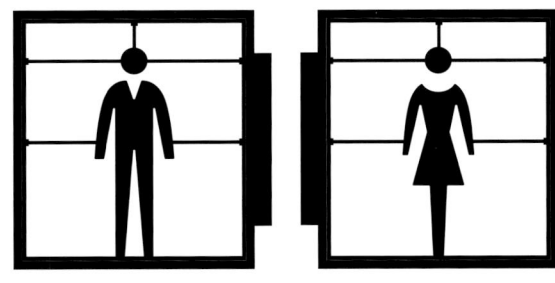

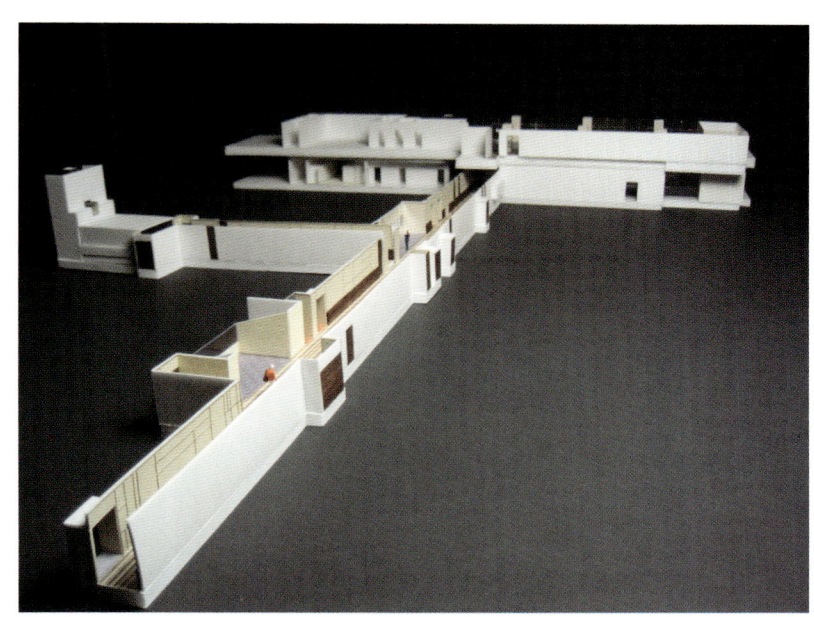

Strata That Decorate a Skyscraper

The Brillia Tower in Tokyo is a 29-storey skyscraper. The specification was for luxurious residential units, which included courtyard gardens and four different types of lounge. Creating a sense of originality are the many different variations on the floor plan of the individual apartments, giving residents a sense of autonomy within the vast building. Intentionallies designed the communal spaces in the upmarket residential high-rise, including the entrance, hallway and lounges.

Although the firm did not work on the whole façade, the team designed and coordinated a series of colour combinations that appears as decoration on the building. The firm had the undersides of the balconies painted in a palette of earth tones. The yellows and browns appear as horizontal layers, and provide a variety in the layering effect which makes up a colour chart that, says Shuwa Tei, 'Expresses, in geological layers, the earth tones of the building,' which is, after all, anchored to the ground, and 'contrasts them with the blue tones of the sky.'

The Evolution of Design Fashioned by Time

Intentionallies

The Evolution of Design Fashioned by Time

Intentionallies

The Shibaura Bloom Tower is located on Shibaura Island, overlooking Tokyo Bay. It is one of four high-rise blocks on the canal-encircled islet, and it was the last of the four buildings to be constructed. Intentionallies was brought in to design the tower's public spaces. At 48 storeys high and containing 1,000 residential units, the scale of the project was enormous. In addition, as the residents vary in age from young families to retired couples – a project objective was to provide housing for a mix of generations – the communal spaces had to be versatile in order to accommodate the wide-ranging needs of the residents.

The concept Intentionallies developed for the public spaces was 'integrated beauty', and the firm categorized the communal areas into three zones. The first of these is the entry zone, where the second-floor entrance hall, corridor and library are viewed as one sequence, with a double-height vaulted ceiling accentuated by orderly rows of columns. The architectural rhythm of the pillars is offset by an expansive view over the surrounding area.

The second zone is a windowless, yet organic space called Laputa Patio. Situated on the 31st floor, it extends seven storeys high. The third zone centres on the Bloom Lounge, also located on the 31st floor. The Bloom Lounge could almost be considered as the grand finale of the building as its doors swing open to reveal, beyond magnificent walls of glass, a panoramic view of Tokyo Bay and the Metropolitan Expressway sweeping towards the city centre.

The building boasts spacious and luxurious communal areas that offer a far higher specification than the average rental accommodation. In order to accent the sequence of the shared areas, Intentionallies added details and flourishes, creating a sense of anticipation. Shuwa Tei explains, 'We paid the utmost attention to the subtle differences in the shades, tones and lustre of the materials. Not only did we use different materials alongside each other, but we also put similar materials with slightly different finishes together, to emphasize their individual qualities. In this way, the space becomes cohesive but at the same time, there is a continuous metamorphosis.'

Intentionallies designed all the furniture and furnishings installed in the communal areas, using durable materials hand-crafted by skilled furniture makers. Relief applied to the walls; woven, lace-like lighting and rhythmically-patterned louvres are brought together in the foyer to shape an interconnected space. Elsewhere, in one of the reception rooms, Intentionallies applied an etching to the stainless steel doors of consoles. A striking bas-relief was applied to the furniture in the main lounge, where the firm also positioned sculptures. Tei elaborates, 'Although we really focused on the details, we also went to great lengths to ensure the narrative remained coherent throughout.' The boldly designed result presents the residents of the tower with a unified feel throughout the entire building.

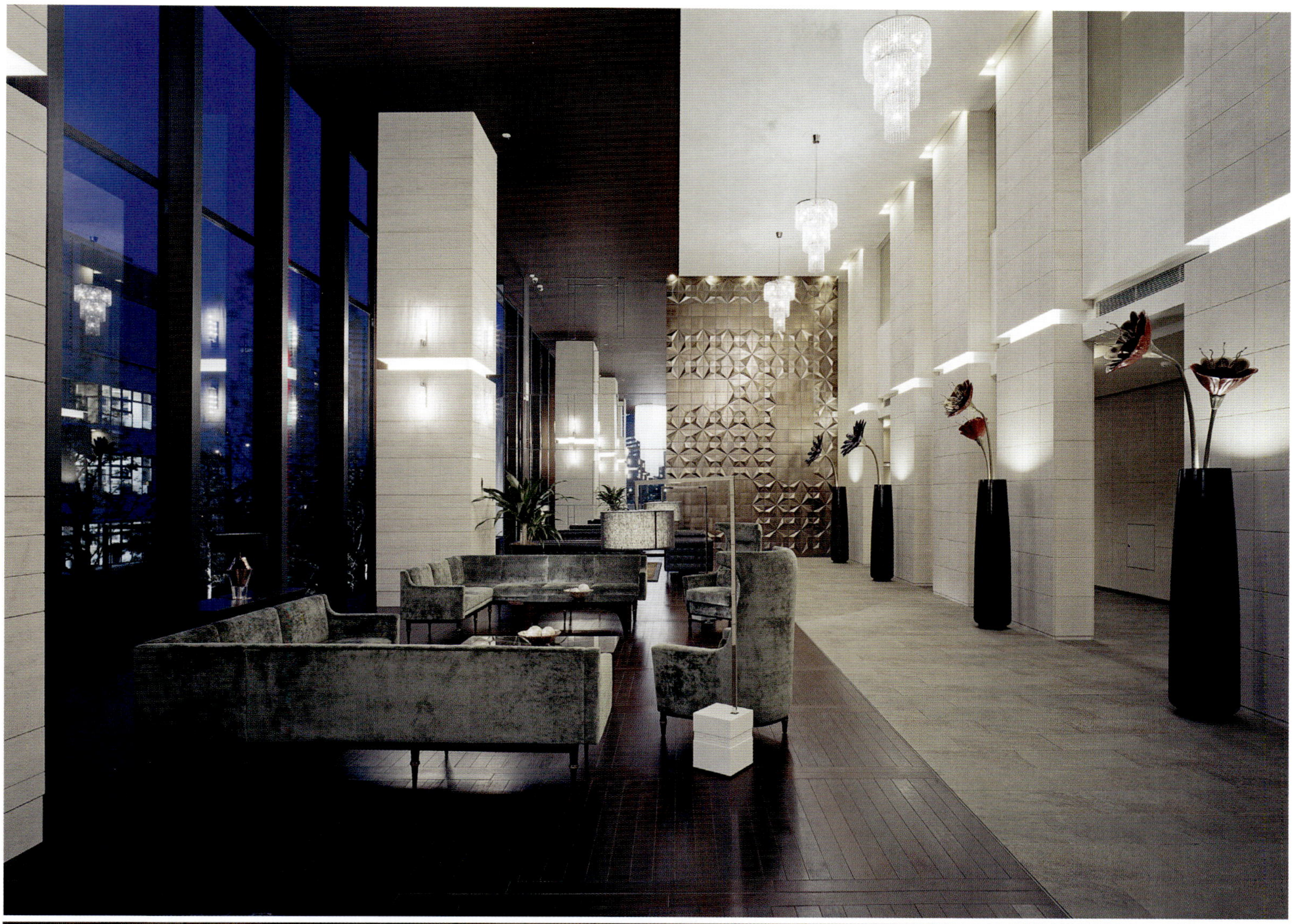

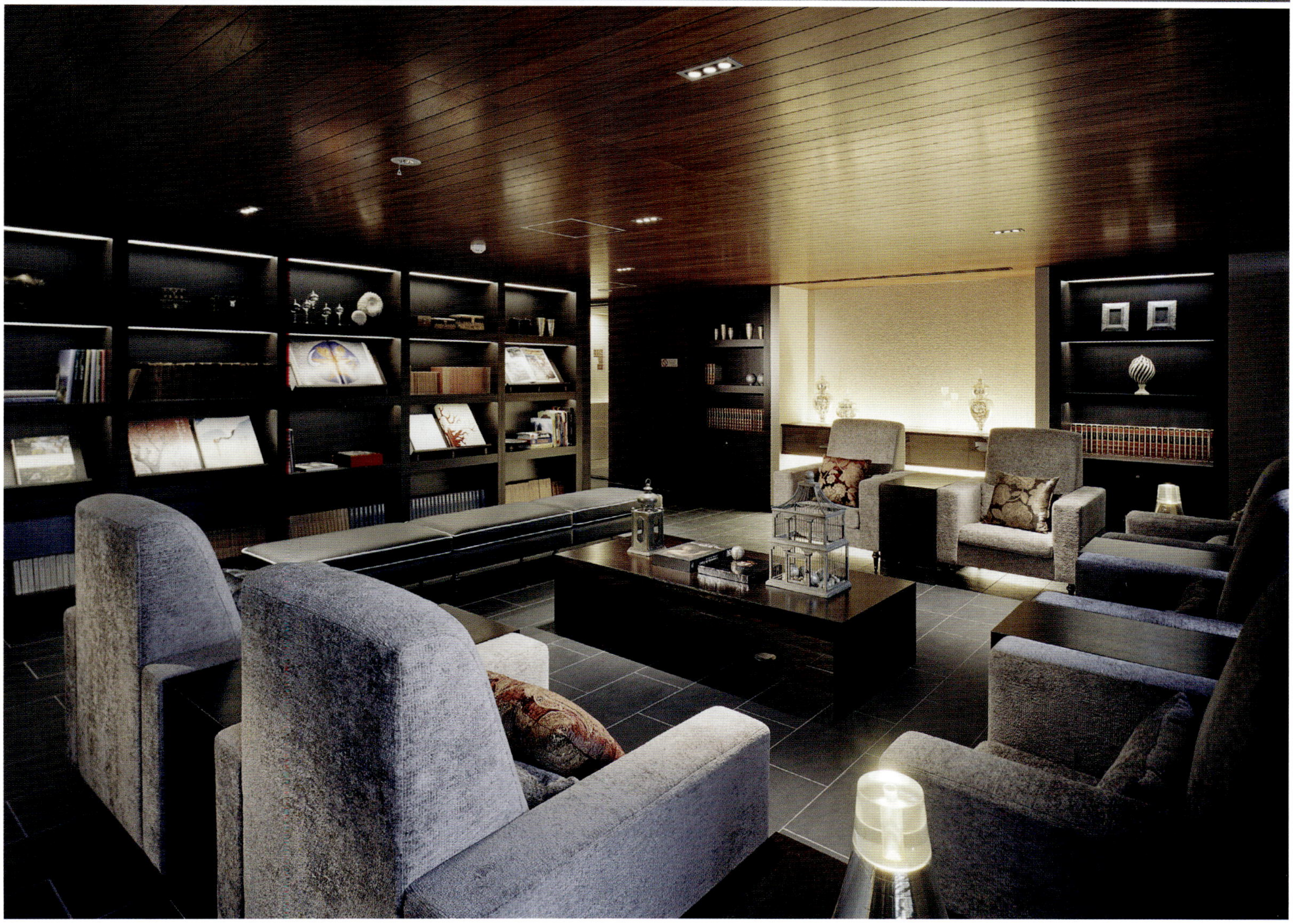

Intentionallies   The Evolution of Design Fashioned by Time

The Evolution of Design Fashioned by Time

Intentionallies

Regionalism:
an Architectural Style That Reflects
the Location of the Project

Intentionallies selected a scenic spot in China for the Hangzhou project. The resort is protected by a river to the front and by a mountain range to the rear. Access to the location is limited, as the only route in is by boat. The site features original Hangzhou architecture, known for its unique 'horse-head' gables. Intentionallies' plan was to renovate the existing building and transform it into a complex with a lounge, restaurant and accommodation for the visitors who come to the area to enjoy its waterways. The development extends from the main building to villas available for rent up-river, and to privately owned villas downstream.

The aim of any architect working on a resort project is ultimately to design a space that enhances a guest's experience of the surrounding area. Intentionallies' method was to work with the local architecture, but at the same time practise ways to create unique qualities for each villa that reflected the local environment. Guests do not come to visit the villas, but rather to experience the scenery of the secluded area. Vital to the success of the project was to cultivate an authentic atmosphere, generated by the architecture created.

All rooms in the villas have a view, either looking out across the open landscape or with a private view onto a beautifully designed courtyard. This was Intentionallies' architectural response to the ambience of the resort and guests' reasons to be there. There are six types of villa, each offering a unique way to interact with nature whether located on the riverfront, in the woods, in a large courtyard or surrounding a pond where the views extend down to the river. The plot is narrow which could have presented Intentionallies with a challenge as the firm needed to secure a footpath around the development without cutting into the space required for the buildings. Intentionallies' solution was to create a maze-like indoor path that connects the different functions of the complex.

The Evolution of Design Fashioned by Time   Intentionallies

Recycling Materials from a Dismantled Building

Declining birth rates meant a primary school, located in woodland near the source of the Tone River, was compelled to merge with a bigger school in the nearest town. Adjacent to the abandoned school was the holiday house of a client of Intentionallies who had week-ended at the house for over 25 years. The client heard about the closure and following discussions, Intentionallies was invited to submit a proposal which would use the empty school in a way that would revitalize the area.

The site is located across the river from a national park with Mount Tanigawa in the distance so Intentionallies presented a concept for a holiday resort. It would consist of 10 villas, an Italian restaurant, a small farm to supply the kitchen with fresh produce, a reception area and a lounge. The resort would take full advantage of food grown locally, create employment opportunities, and host workshops for primary school children. It was Intentionallies' objective to create a complex that local residents would love.

The firm understood that as the school had been there for 100 years, there were strong emotional ties to it, and the team could

imagine how difficult it would be for the local people to see the beloved school buildings being torn down. To mitigate this, Intentional-lies decided to recycle the reinforced concrete parts of the old structures by having them crushed to provide material for the founda-tions of the roadbed, finishing material for pavements and heat insulation for the roofs of the new buildings. Therefore the old building would be partly metamorphosed into the new, preserving much of its spirit.

Intentionallies worked with the principles that had been established for the developments the firm had worked on in Bali, using the 'echord' values, which included incorporating sustainable approaches and clean energy. The recycling of the old school not only reduced the volume of waste material usually generated during a reconstruction, but also ensured the locals felt included in the estab-lishment of the new project.

A Peninsula Ripe for Development

Indonesia

Bali Island

• Negara

The Evolution of Design Fashioned by Time

Intentionallies

The Negara district, on Bali's west coast, is a rare sight on the Indonesian island as the area has not been developed as a resort, even though it's the second largest conurbation after Denpasar. With the number of visitors to Bali predicted to rise over the coming years, the district would be the perfect location for a new resort. At the tip of the peninsula is a particularly beautiful area called Perancak, a spot that Intentionallies earmarked as the ideal location to develop a string of high-end resorts.

From the ocean-fronting sites, the views are incredible. Across the sea, the island of Java is just about visible in the far distance. The beaches fronting the properties are serene and tranquil, dotted with pretty little fishing boats moored close to the shore. Fresh from the ocean, the daily catch ranges from tuna and sardines to shrimps, crabs and sea urchins. From the properties located alongside the lagoon, visitors have views of the ebb and flow of the tidal river, the green carpet of the mangroves and clusters of pristine palm trees on the far shore. In the distance are the jungle-covered mountains of the National Park. Less than one hour's drive is an internationally acclaimed spot for diving and a hot springs spa. Visitors taking a trip out to sea by boat can expect to see dolphins and whales, at the right time of year. In addition, the beaches in front of the resorts are a popular spot for sea turtles to head to, to lay their eggs.

Intentionallies is developing three projects in the area. All three were devised using the same approach, namely, by establishing a sense of regionalism in the architectural projects by exploring the context and heritage of the location, by implementing sustainable principles and developing an 'echord'.

What is 'echord'?
The word echord is derived from two almost contradictory words, ecology and economy. These words both come from the Greek word *oikos*, which means house in English. As Intentionallies sees these two words combining to distil the ethos of its aims in the construction of these villas in Bali, the firm has coined the new word 'echord' to convey the meaning wished for.

ec
[conj.] an irregular form of eco- (ecology). biology, environment, biogeocenos, [for or of] environmental conservation
[abbr.] economy, saving, thrift, economic, business activity

echo
[noun] the repetition of a sound caused by the reflection of a sound wave; the reverberation of a sound or voice in mountainous regions

chord
[noun] three or more musical tones sounded simultaneously
[noun] empathy
[noun] heart strings, sensibility

Establishing Regionalism in an Architectural Project Through Context and Heritage

Water splashes down through a series of terraced swimming pools that symbolize the relationship between the W-residence and the ocean. The design language of the project found a perfect balance between traditional – for example, alang alang-roofing – Balinese aesthetics and a distinguished modern style. The complex consists of a group of independent luxury bungalows, each with different panoramas from the windows: an ocean view, a garden view or a picturesque combination of the two.

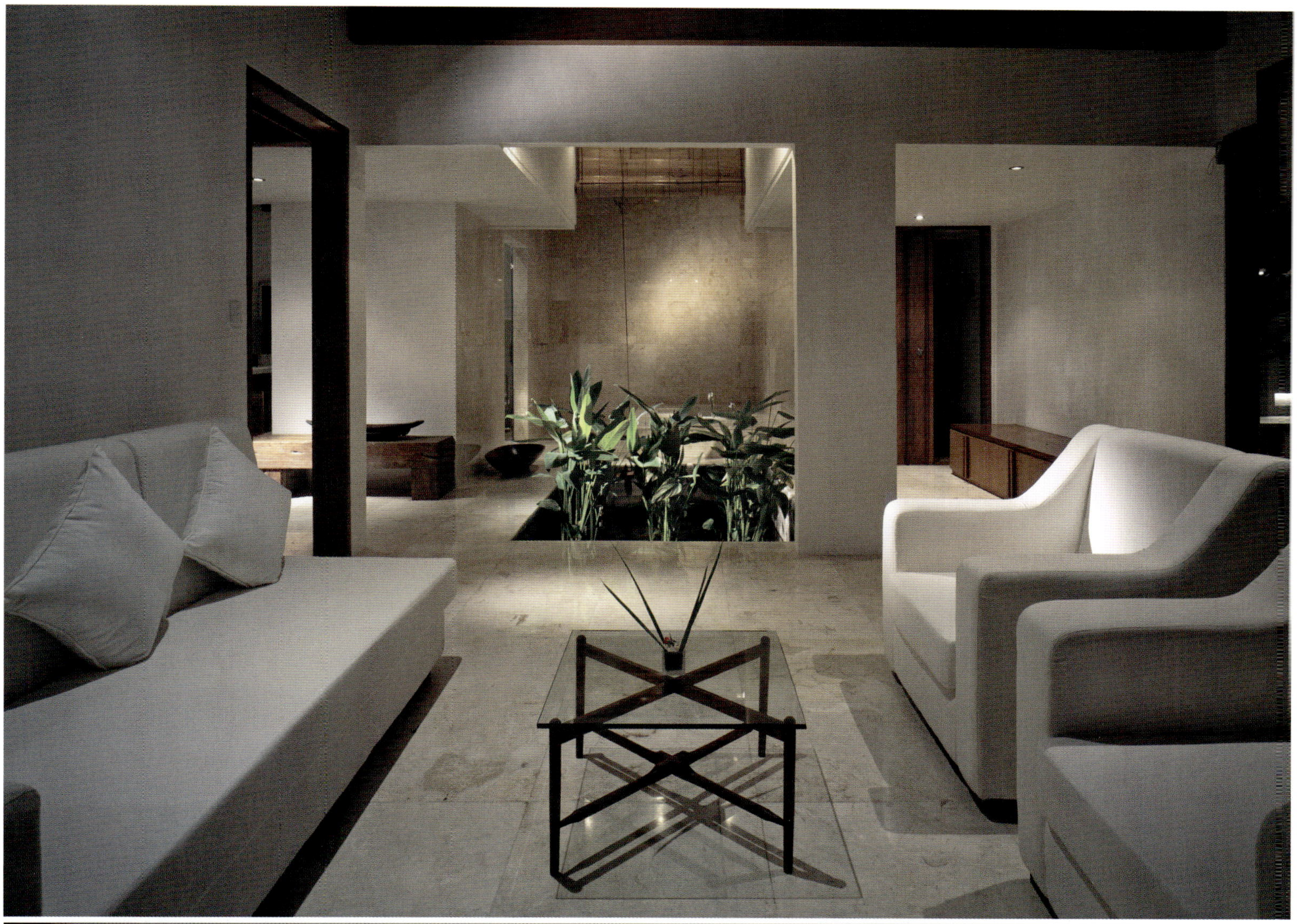

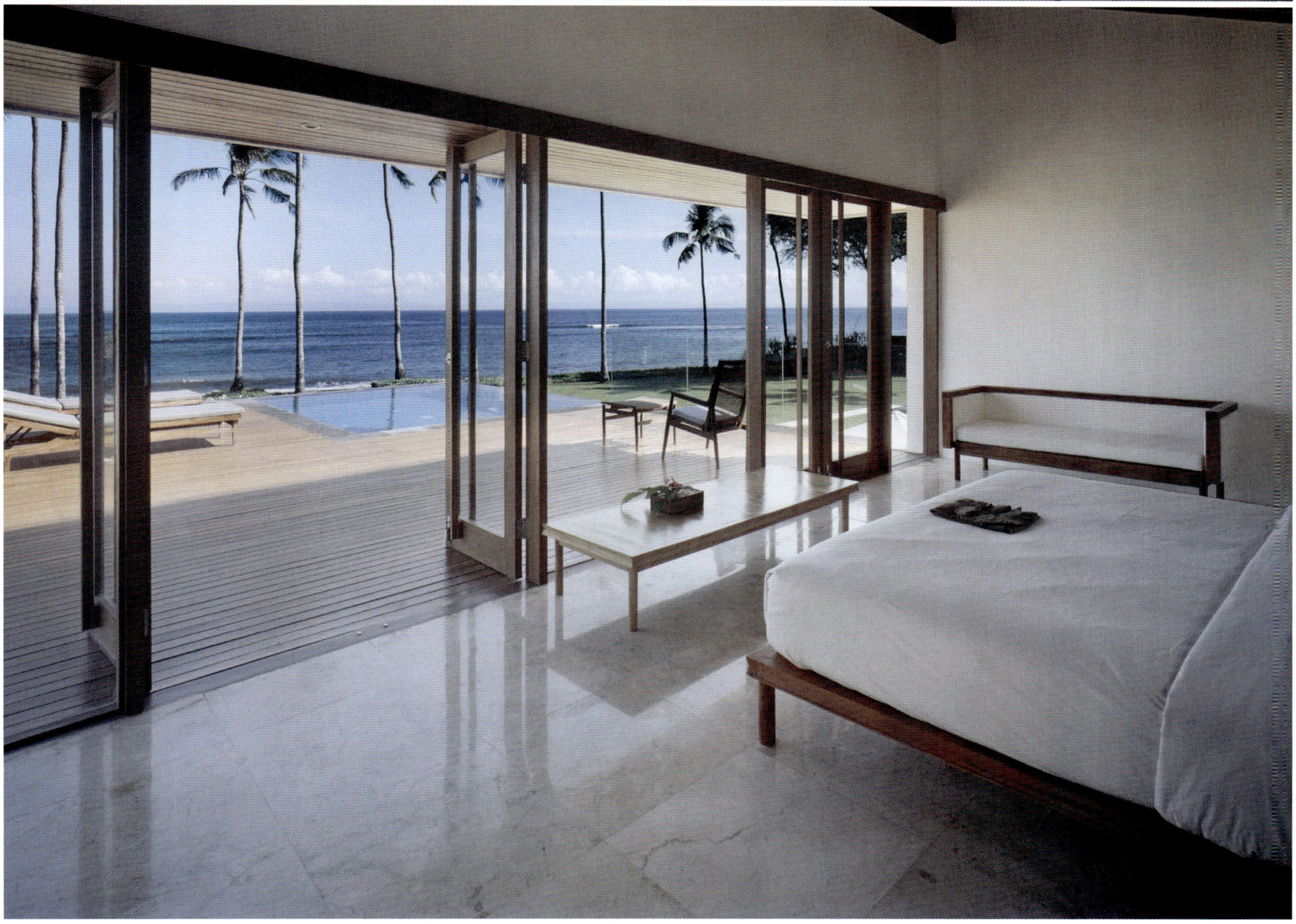

A Holiday Complex Connected by Waterways

The project comprises a series of villas that are connected by a cascade of pools and channels that are arranged throughout the site and have a combined length of 100 m. The waterways lead down to the beach, where the pools give a view towards the infinity of the ocean. Water falling from one level to the next, from one pool to the next, not only cools the buildings, but also provides a soothing backdrop of sight and sound. The innovation in this complex is the connection of levels and elevations by water.

The layout for each location is different. The Garden Villa is characterized by a large sloping roof with bedrooms laid out symmetrically with gardens on all four sides. The Pool Villa has a living room that is mainly glazed and opens out to a pool. The Ocean Front Villa has a two-story foyer, adding more height to the building. It is the nearest to the ocean; between the house and the sea, and connecting the two, is a Jacuzzi. The Master Villa is defined by its extensive ground floor, which measures 15 x 15 m and is enclosed by glass. The pool attached to the property is 15 m long and is open to the ocean. The architectural forms and the private areas within the structures are uniquely tied to nature.

Shuwa Tei says, 'We consider that the completion of the construction of the complex is just the beginning, as the materials will weather and take on a new texture, and the gardens will mature. We wanted the whole complex to take on a vintage appearance.' Intentionallies invested in the local Balinese furniture-making industries, employing local artisans who would make furniture for the villas working to the firm's designs, and teaching them, where necessary, how to make the more complex pieces.

The architectural features accentuate the beauty of straight lines. For contrast, various decorative pieces incorporating curves are spread around. Shrubs that will mature over time are strategically placed. Intentionallies will continue to develop the landscaping and furnishings. Tei adds, 'Once we begin to feel the warmth and presence of the people who gather there, we will have an early view of how successful our designs have been. As time passes, we would like to make further improvements to the complex.'

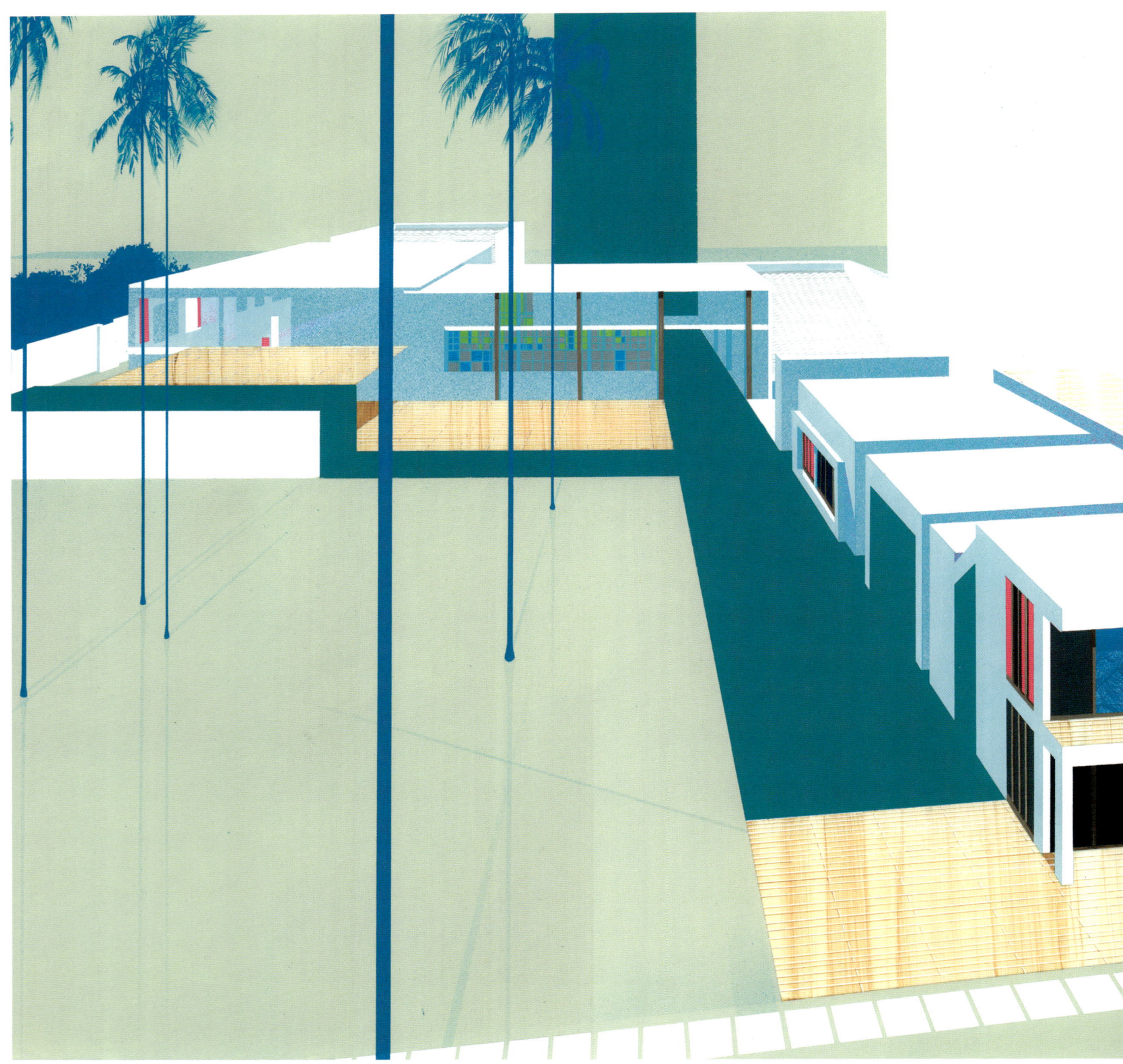

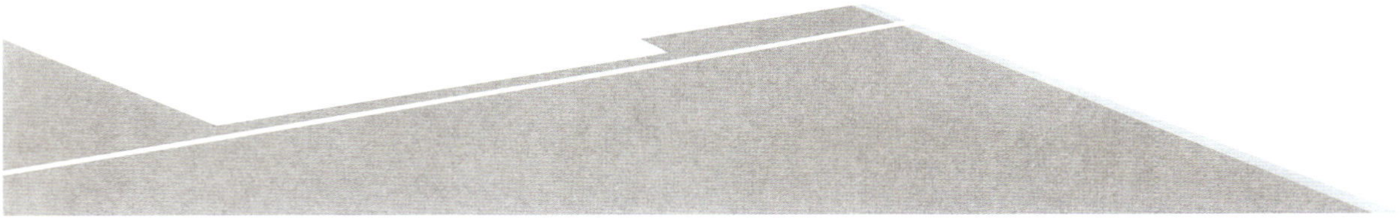

Using Water to Integrate a Group of Buildings

Another of Intentionallies' objectives, applied also to other villa projects in Bali, was to provide a quiet and serene atmosphere with only the sound of the waves of the sea, with nothing to worry about, with time to look at the ocean, in the shade feeling a cool breeze or with sunlight on the skin. The ultimate goal is to create a place that provides such precious moments.

The SGM Villa project consists of three buildings connected by a common area that is clearly separated from the private areas around each building. Three pools, each at a slightly lower level than the one before, lie parallel with the buildings. Water cascades gently and soothingly from one pool to the next. As in the case of the ITL Villa, water plays a crucial role in linking and uniting the structures in both plan and elevation.

As guests enter the gate they are greeted by a water basin that seems to stretch out to the ocean, preparing them for the spaciousness to come.

The main building lies behind a large pond and tall trees, stressing privacy and separation from the guest buildings. The living and dining area with its high, vaulted ceiling is the main feature of the building. It has two 12-m wide openings that seem to unite it with the surroundings.

Two separate guest buildings complete the complex. One has two storeys, with a private pool directly outside the living area, and a bedroom above with an expansive view of the ocean, providing quite different views from each floor. The other building has a sprawling layout with a 10-m pool, outdoor living space

that extends to 100 m², indoor living spaces, and a bedroom. By bringing views of the outdoors into the interior, the entire space feels expansive. By giving each independent area generous views, Intentionallies has successfully incorporated the beauty of the surrounding natural elements into the essence of the luxury bungalows that form SGM Villa.

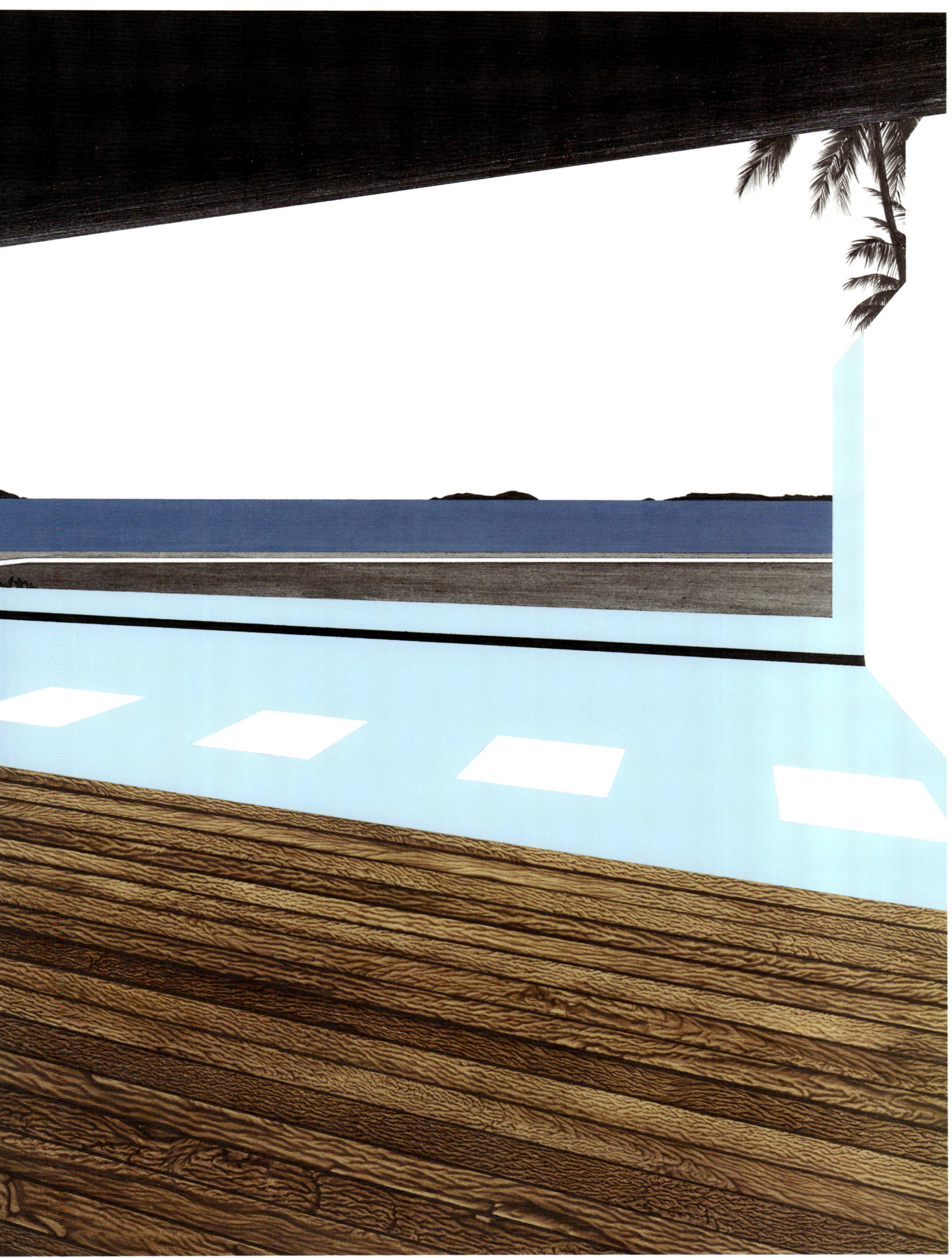

Process of evolution in architectural style with regionalism

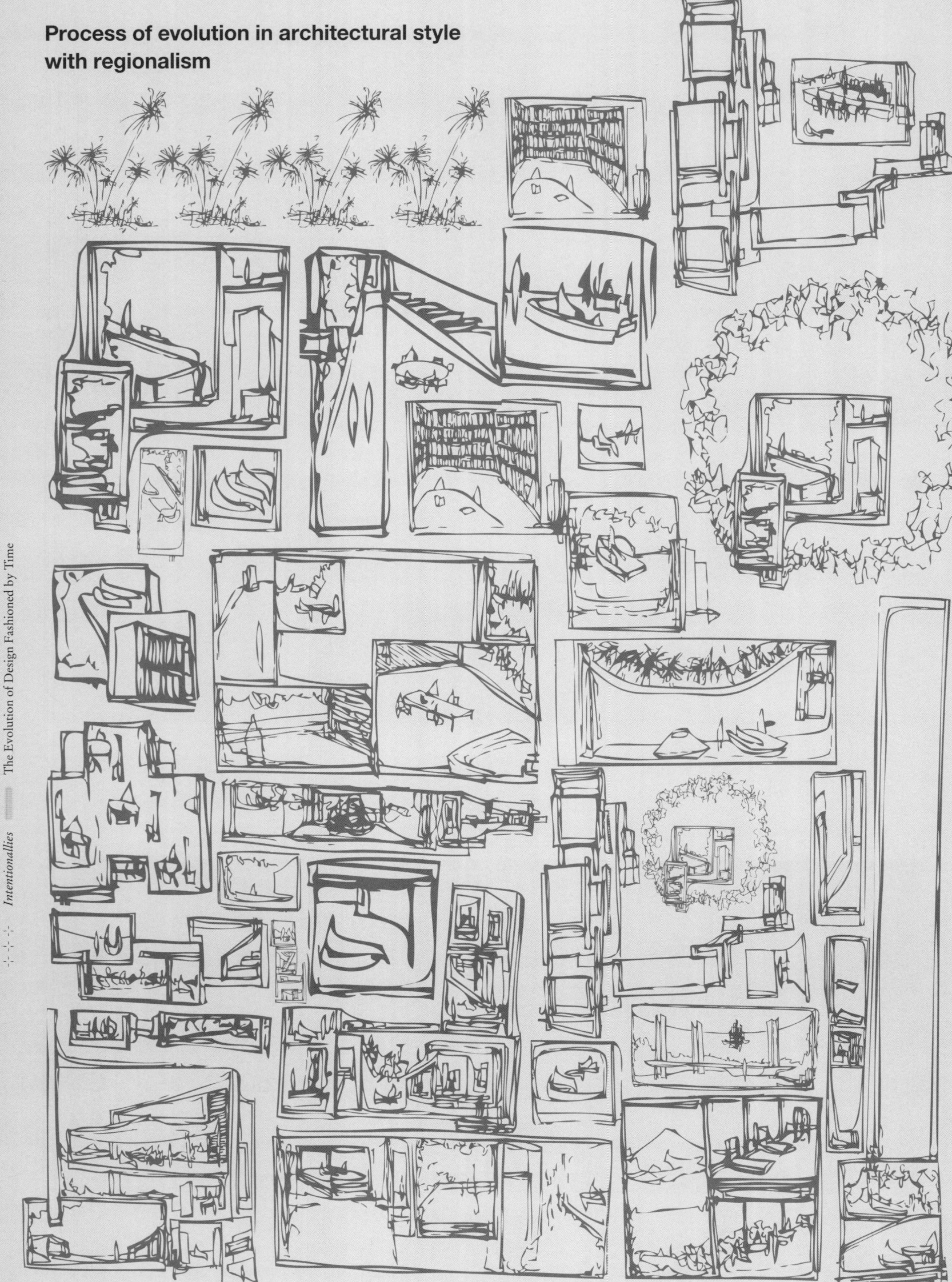

Lagoon villa

Ocean Front villa

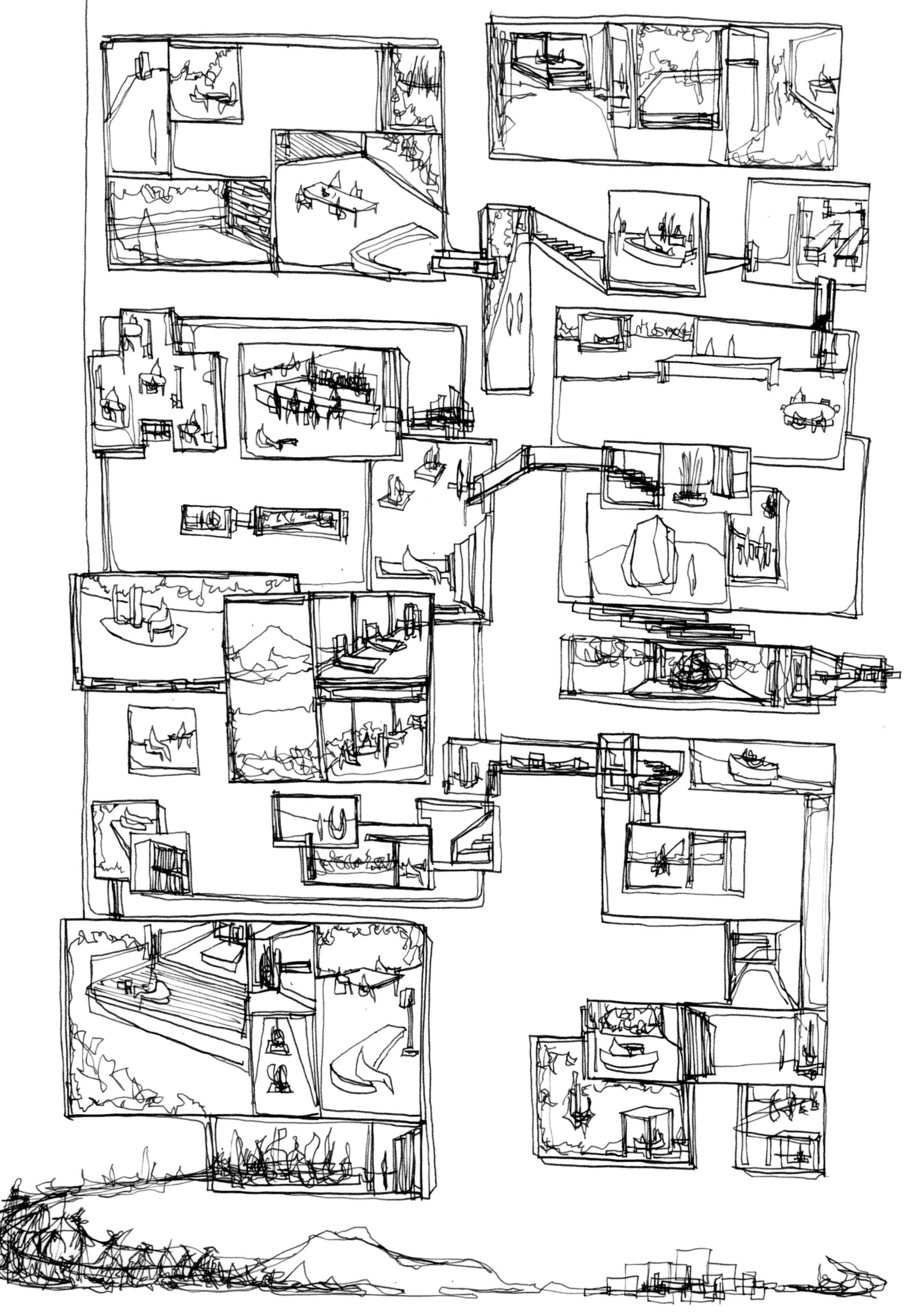

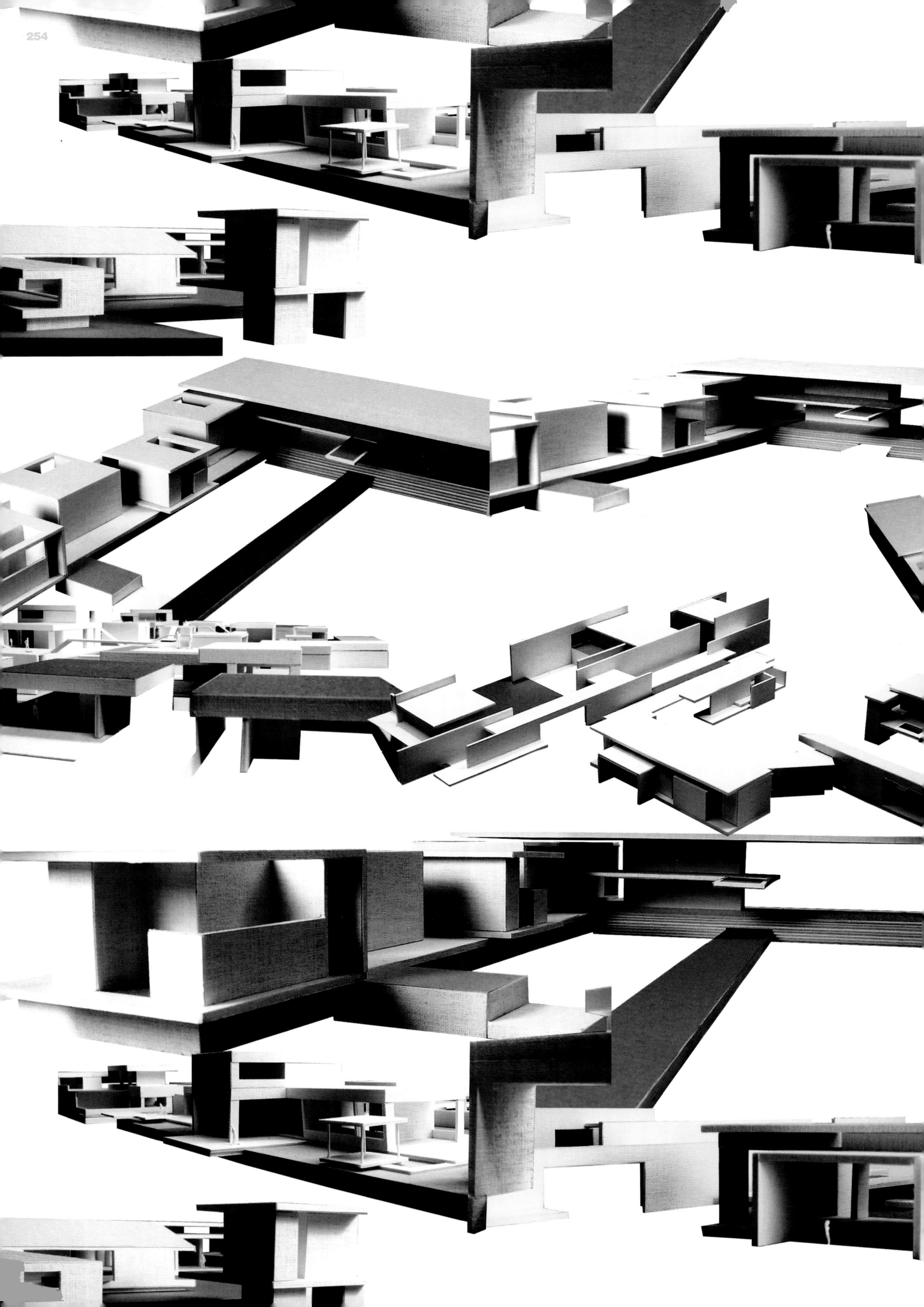

ITL Lagoon villa

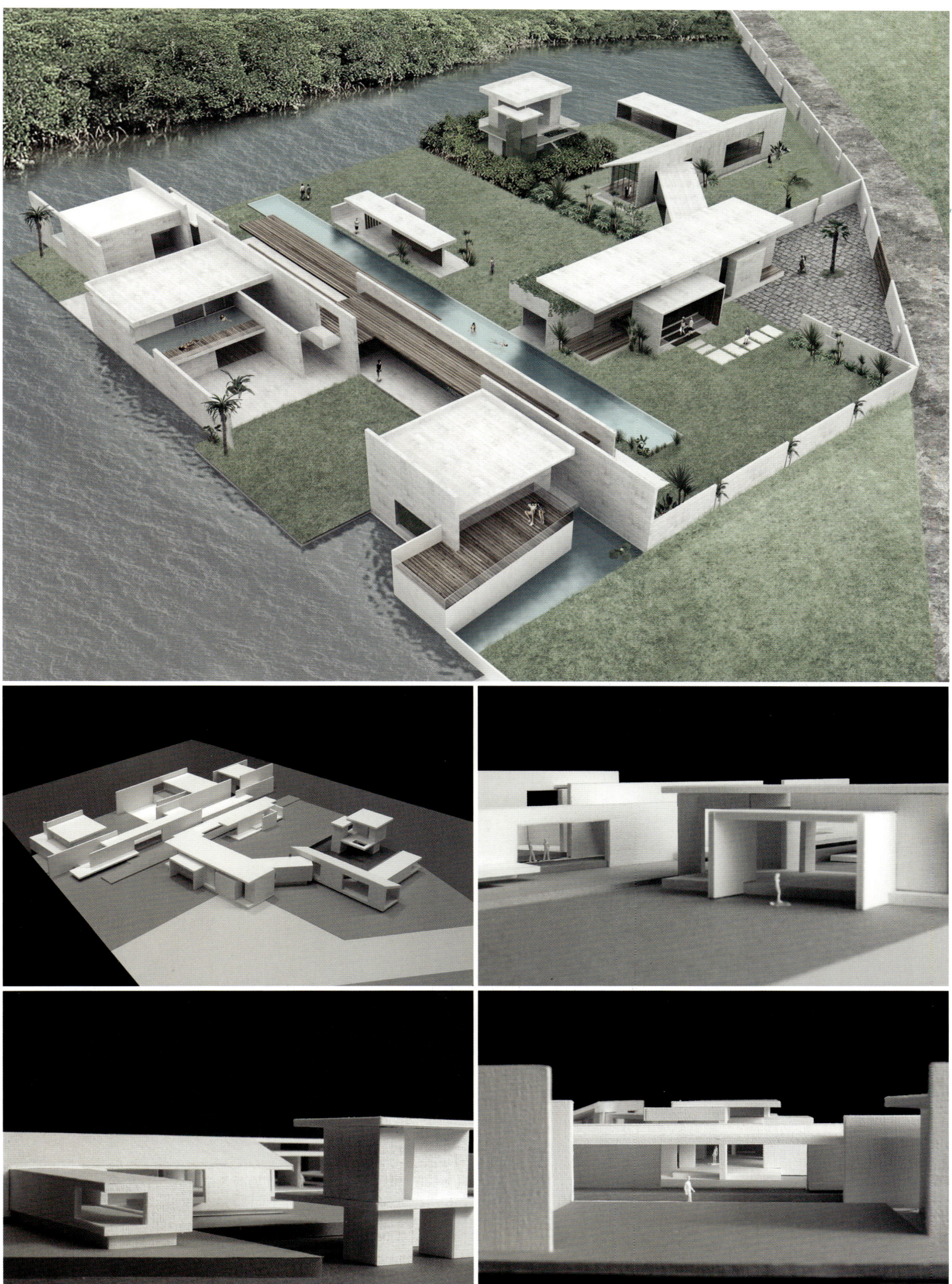

Creating a New Urban Area

Shuwa Tei says, 'The way urban areas are being formed is dramatically different from the past. We can now forecast that circumstances are more unpredictable than ever. Mobile devices have changed the way people relate to their local area and the way they make commitments. Furthermore, dramatic changes have been brought to methods of communication. Methods of work are changing too: a designer no longer sharpens a pencil and sits at a drafting table with tracing paper but instead, faces a computer screen. Much of what once required going physically to a site, modifying a drawing, sharing information, or obtaining data concerning it, can now be done with the click of a mouse. We've always wanted to find our own solution as to how we can instantly make a connection with and commit ourselves to a hectically changing urban environment. In some cities we are exploring the possibility of supplying clean electrical energy throughout by 2010. While we believe that realizing this goal at Haneda Airport may be difficult, we think that it could be done under licence in other cities. I say this with conviction because of our successful experience in facing challenges in many different parts of the globe. This is the world as we see it: exploring consumer electronics is part of the architectural design process. Creating the amadana line from the ground upwards was the first step in our participation in the formation of future urban areas. With this credo we look forward to taking the fullest possible part in the construction of the urban areas of the future.'

**A Residential Complex
That Expresses an Elevated
Standard of Living**

A Tower Decorated in the Binary Scale

The Farglory U-Town project was started over 25 years ago when the building of infrastructure such as roads and tram routes was begun in greater Taipei to establish a new suburb. During that time period, changing circumstances resulted in the project being modified. Intentionallies had initially been invited to design the interior of a lounge in the Farglory U-Town building. However, the firm made a presentation that emphasized the importance of integrating its design into the overall concept of the building. In preparation, the team had carefully and thoroughly examined the progress of the project as it had evolved during the 25-year period.

Intentionallies suggested that the building be located in the centre of the city in order to house family-run businesses and small factories. The firm felt that a key element of the project was to expand the collective business by encouraging the small businesses housed in the building to network. In its design concept for the project, Intentionallies was inspired by the fact that the ancestry of the president of the company could be traced back to the Chinese Han dynasty. The concept of yin and yang, the dark and light symbol of the Han people, is parallel to the Western concept of zero and one. Zero and one have evolved into the binary scale that is used in computer languages in the modern age. With the background information, with the development over time and with the consideration of the fact that Taiwan is known as the world centre of digital device production, Intentionallies decided that it was fitting to design the façades of the building so that they would show the binary numeral system using dark and light glass panels. Instead of simply using zero and one, the firm would portray the infinite possibilities of binary mathematics in forming the decoration of the façades in complicated puzzles, enumerations and notations.

When complete, the tower will become a landmark for Taipei in the 21st century. Intentionallies is convinced that the decoration of the building using the binary numeral system will be a great success.

Creating a New Urban Area

Intentionallies

The Identity of the City of Taipei

The Farglory Taipei Dome is a project on a massive scale; discussions were first initiated over 10 years ago. Before Intentionallies joined the design team, there had been no overall, unifying design concept and once on board, Intentionallies felt it was immediately necessary to establish a master plan.

A stadium is often considered the main building in a city area, withhotels, commercial buildings and offices located around it. However, when Intentionallies analysed the business scheme of the Farglory Dome, the firm realized that establishing a connection between the stadium and the surrounding facilities was urgent. Intentionallies placed special emphasis on how the firm could connect people

to people, people to facilities, and facilities to facilities. In addition, the firm searched for a fitting conceptual theme. Taiwan has had a long history of exporting butterflies, and butterflies are considered auspicious. After much consideration, Intentionallies decided to name the dome the 'Taipei Butterfly Field' and to use butterflies as the design motif to unify the buildings surrounding the stadium. The landscape beyond is also in the process of being transformed into a biotope that will provide a habitat primarily for butterflies. The urban planning schemes that Intentionallies proposed have resulted in the firm taking a leading role in the project, steering the architectural design offices involved.

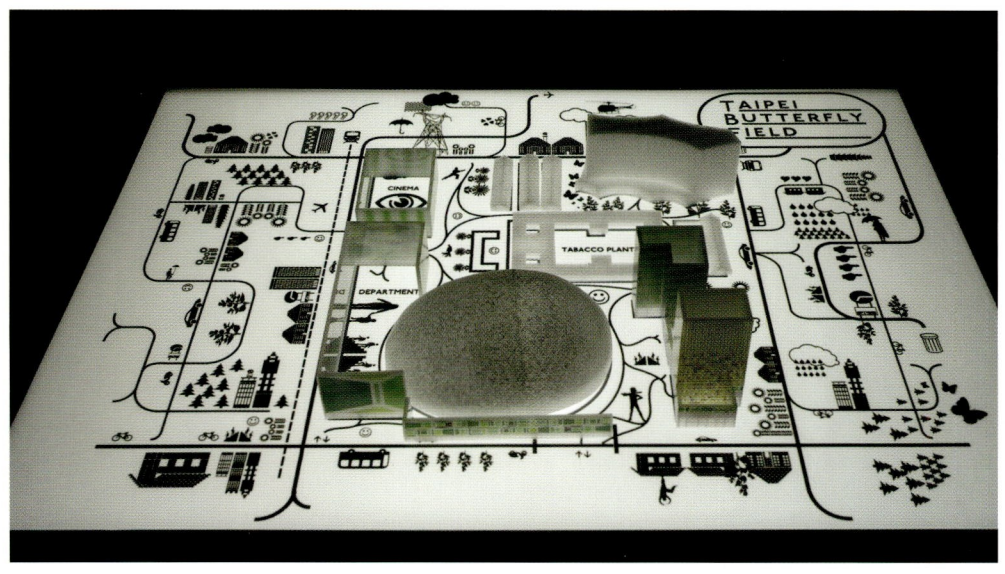

Intentionallies

Creating a New Urban Area

TAIPEI
BUTTERFLY
FIELD

CINEMA

HOTEL, OFFICE &SHOP

OLD FACTORY

DECK TERRACE

DEPARTMENT

DOME

OFFICE

HOTEL

MALL

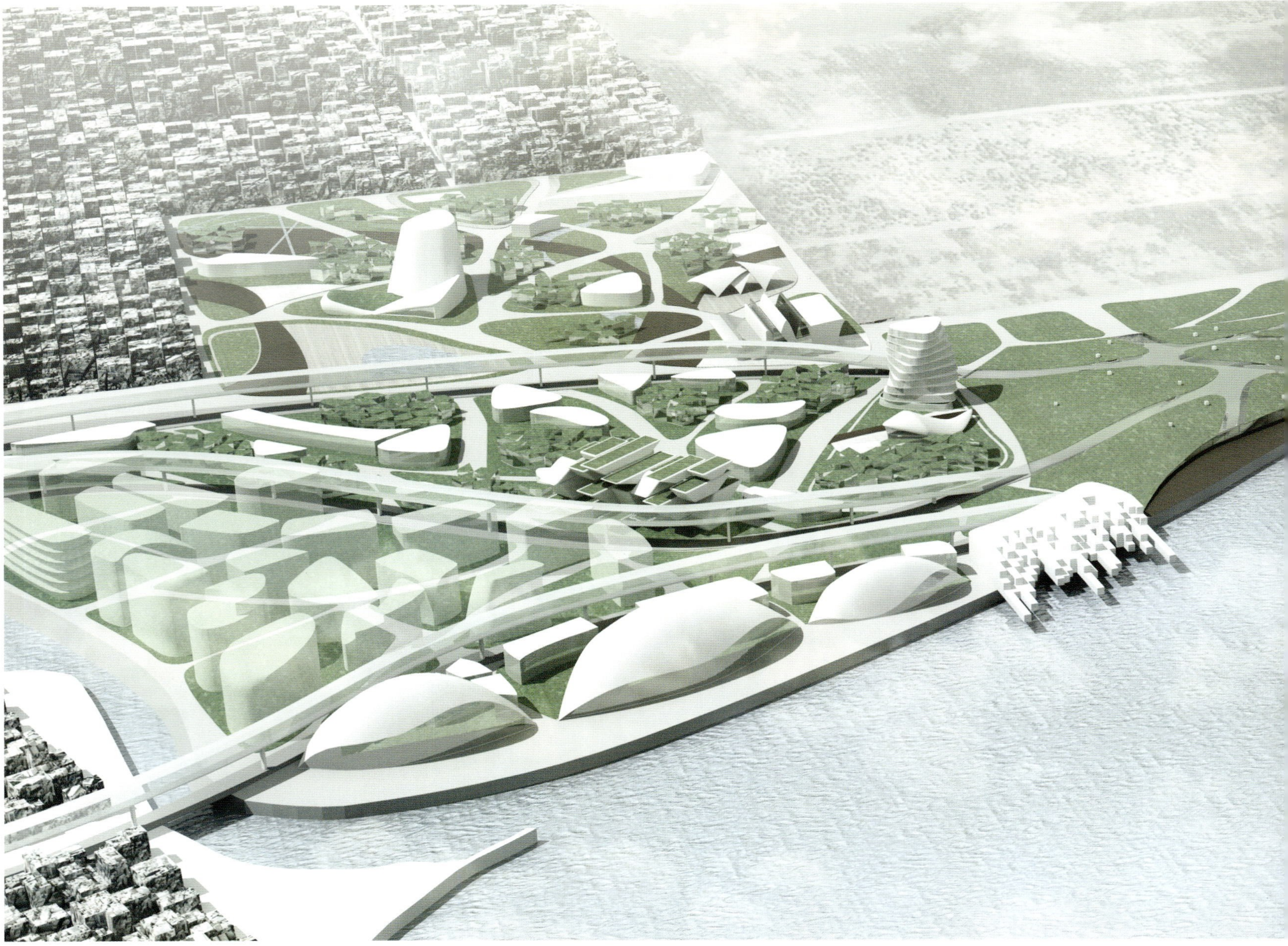

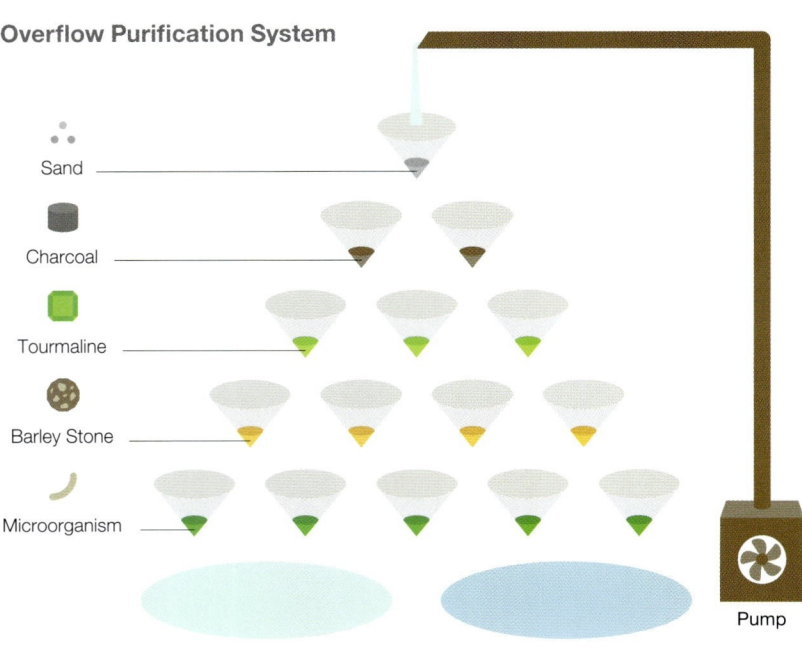

Creating a New Urban Area

Intentionallies

Wind Power
Generation

Wave Activated
Power Generation

Photovoltaic
Generation

Geothermal
Power Generation

Overflow Purification System

Sand

Charcoal

Tourmaline

Barley Stone

Microorganism

Pump

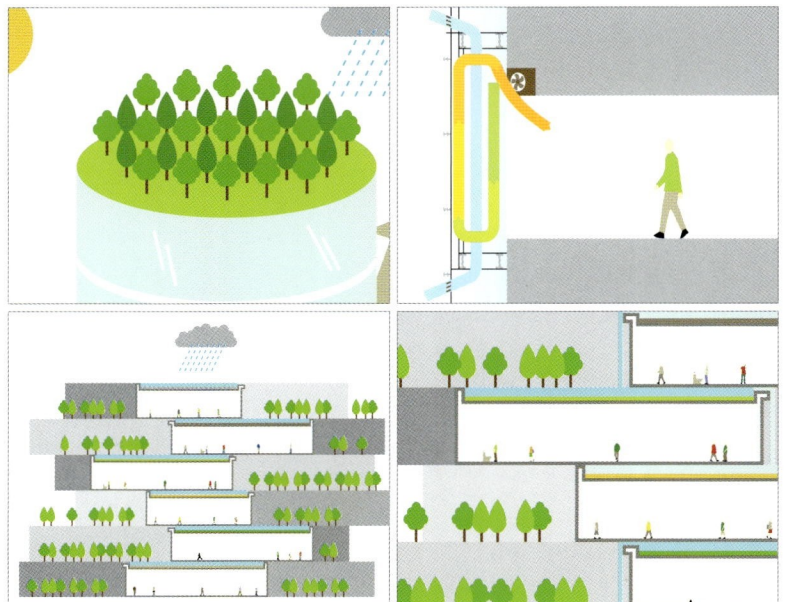

The Distillation of the Real Needs of Urban Planning for the Future Using the Most Advanced Technology

'We believe that a city in the 21st century must develop an optimized energy network based upon green energy,' says Shuwa Tei. 'Depending on the environmental conditions, solar, wind, water, geothermal and biomass power production must be placed in a proper balance throughout the city in order to provide a stable power supply. This optimization includes not only the energy supply but also its distribution. Compact and effective transportation means that approaches such as car or bicycle sharing must be established so that the next generation energy hubs will provide opportunities for new communities to form.'

Tei continues, 'We propose the establishment of the Post Schematic City as a vision of a city in the 21st century, in which nodes proliferate, connect with each other and expand as a network, as with the internet. The nodes will be called EMS (Energy Mileage Stations) and become part of the optimized system for the environment. They are primarily the city's infrastructure charge stations for electric cars, bicycles and buses. Once the next generation high-performance batteries are developed, the buying and selling of power will be done more freely. This will allow for more organic interrelationships between facilities and energy distribution. Buses and cars will be able to stop at an EMS to unload any surplus power. A senior citizen may generate power by pushing a walker cart and then unload the power at the station in exchange for electronic money to go shopping. Tree planting or volunteer work could accrue "mileage". When public facilities are set up at the EMS, new urban entities will come into existence and they will expand.'

EMS Passive Air-flow System

Summer

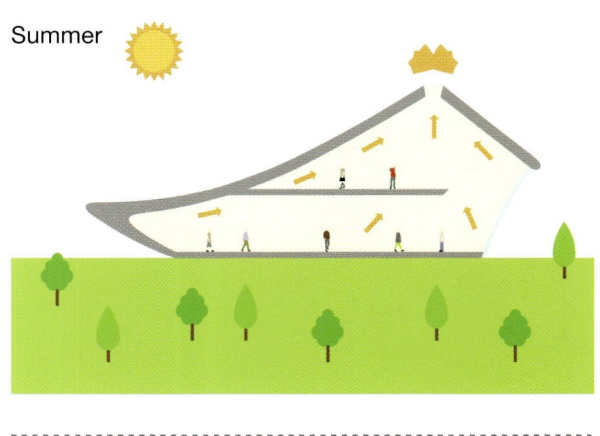

Winter

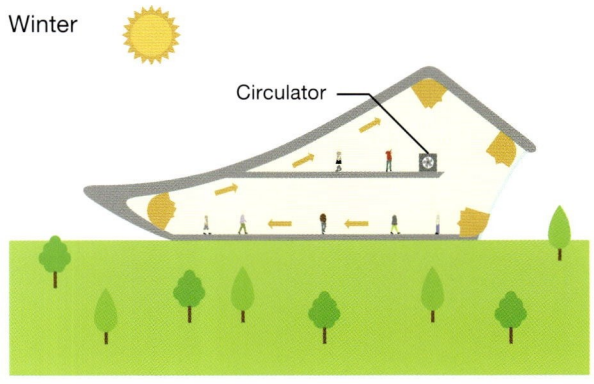

Solar Tube Chandelier

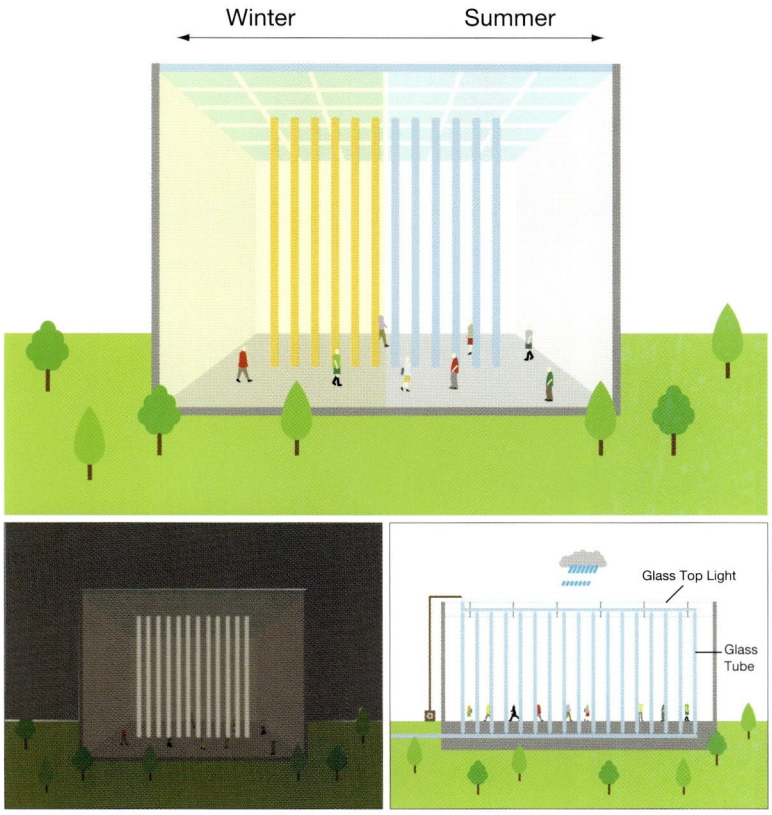

Energy Myrage Station (EMS)

Intentionallies   Everything Towards Creating a New Urban Area

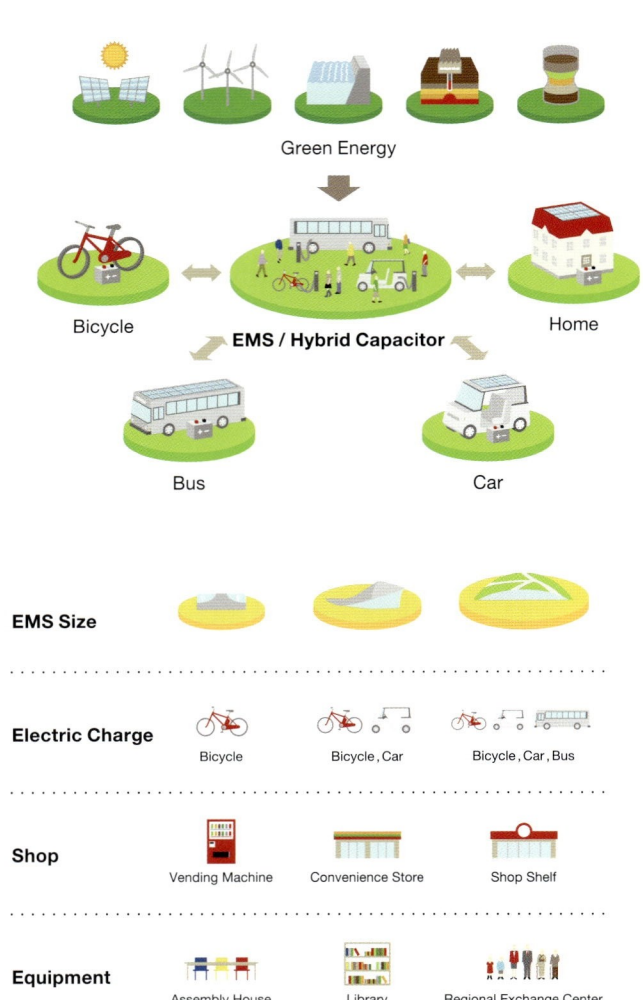

Green Energy

Bicycle

EMS / Hybrid Capacitor

Home

Bus

Car

EMS Size

Electric Charge — Bicycle — Bicycle, Car — Bicycle, Car, Bus

Shop — Vending Machine — Convenience Store — Shop Shelf

Equipment — Assembly House — Library — Regional Exchange Center

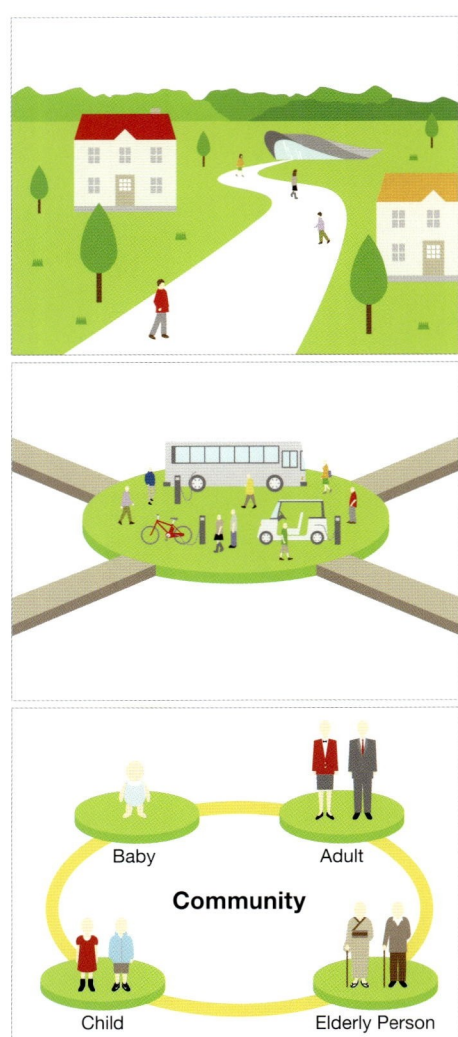

Community

Baby — Adult — Child — Elderly Person

Photovoltaic Generation

Wind Power Generation

Hybrid Capacitor

Biomass Power Generation

Wave Activated Power Generation

Geothermal Power Generation

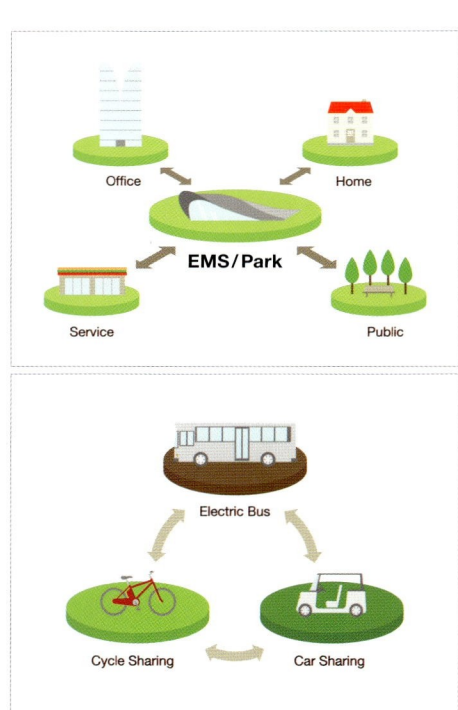

Office — Home

EMS / Park

Service — Public

Electric Bus

Cycle Sharing — Car Sharing

City Structure for 21st century

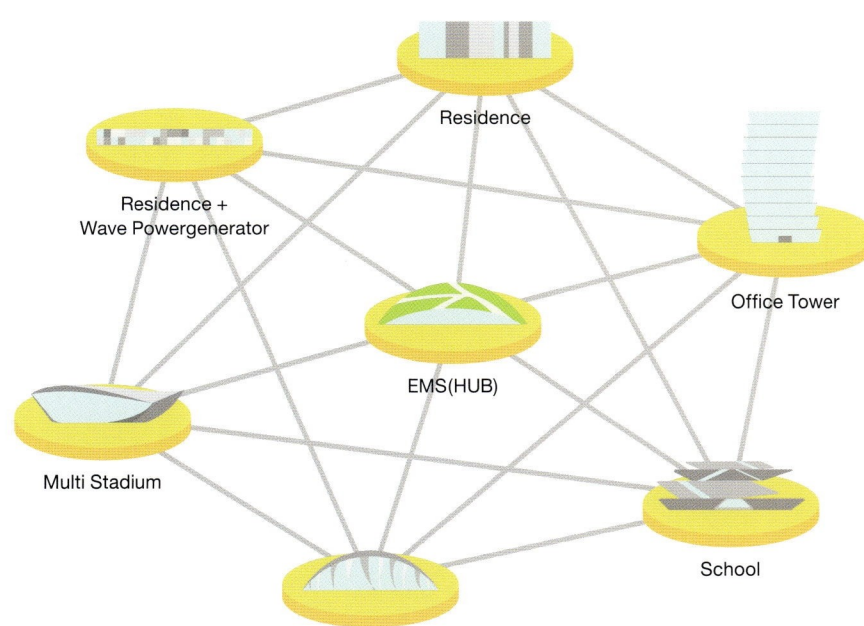

General Hospital

Weltare Institution

EMS

Gate

Library

Residence

Residence +
Wave Powergenerator

Office Tower

EMS(HUB)

Multi Stadium

School

Public Hall Culture

Social Infrastructure by Digital Cash

Digital Cash

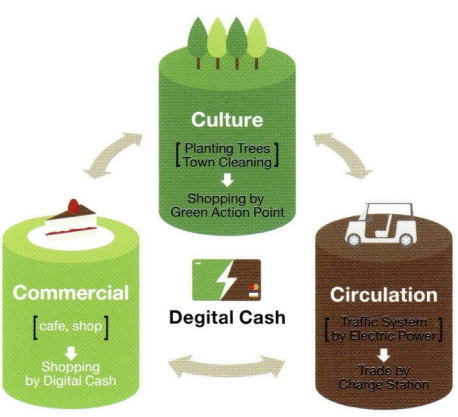

Culture
[Planting Trees]
[Town Cleaning]
↓
Shopping by
Green Action Point

Commercial
[cafe, shop]
↓
Shopping
by Digital Cash

Degital Cash

Circulation
[Traffic System]
[by Electric Power]
↓
Trade by
Charge Station

'We believe that a polyphony (a progression of harmonious parts) unites environment, architecture and mankind as one to create harmony, and that this is what we think a city should be like,' adds Tei. 'We integrated visual representations of Chladni's sound patterns into the architectural designs of the proposal. Meanwhile, the environmentally friendly facility devices form an overflow purification system which channels rainwater and river water down through terraced tiers, purifying the water en route. The water that runs down the tiers can form the background decoration for a room or it may provide heat insulation, serving as an environmental facility as well as a resonating facility.

'In additional, facilities and devices that environmentally support and fuse with other similar facilities such as a heat collecting utility, called a solar tube chandelier, will be widely adopted throughout the city. Furthermore, independent standards for "green" buildings and their certification process will be established in order to provide direction for sustainable operations. We will strive to establish an environmentally friendly urban life cycle by systematically managing the life cycles of urban facilities. We believe that the formation of a city as a Post Schematic City will gradually take place regardless of the region, intended purpose, size or nature. In fact, the formation of a network has already begun in an invisible way. The next step is for us to move on to a higher level of the Post Schematic City.'

The first time I entered the amadana shop in Tokyo's Omotesando Hills I got that rare sensation that I was witnessing a change. Something profound, and with such a revelation comes a second question: 'Is it for the better?' In order to answer that, let's stop and think about the world we live in and Shuwa Tei's and Intentionallies' role in it.

Modern consumer technology often tends to be complicated. So complicated that seemingly simple household appliances require a 200-page manual. Confronted with such a publication, dejection is close at hand and we most likely begin to ask ourselves what it is that we actually need and what products can satisfy our needs, which often tend to be emotional. Flipping through one of those telephone directory-sized manuals can make anyone long for a calculator that is only a calculator, an appliance that knows no other skills than to compute numbers and doesn't pretend to be something else. Plato would probably have said that the amadana calculator represents the idea of a calculator. Intentionallies takes our longing seriously and for amadana, they have designed an entire catalogue of such products. Solid, reliable pieces; household appliances that feel heavy, qualitative and somewhat exclusive, and products that you – on an intuitive level – feel you will be able to operate in the same way that you don't mistrust a Bakelite telephone.

The appeal of the products of Intentionallies' design universe is that they render a certain exclusivity to their owners' lifestyle. The way of life promoted not only by the amadana brand, but also by Craft Design Technology, is one characterized by thoughtfulness. This is a very contemporary notion. An architect friend of mine bought an amadana calculator. Not because he couldn't do without that particular one – some application on his computer might have been equally capable of performing the job – but because certain tasks demand a worthy piece of equipment. In this case, something with a certain weight and tactility. An appliance you have confidence in.

A great paradox of our time is that the desire for solid products and the time, effort and skill needed to make them actually increases when technical developments in a sense has rendered them or the craft obsolete.

It is clear that Intentionallies designs, not only for what Virginia Postrel has dubbed 'the age of look and feel', but for consumers who turn their commitment to sustainability into an interest in the origin and durability of products. If Shuwa Tei's whole approach to design is that you have to take a step back in order to be contemporary, the same can be said of his attitude towards his own profession.

The role of the architect has, in many places, been reduced to that of a consultant among others. It comes as no surprise that one of Shuwa Tei's idols is the Danish architect and designer Arne Jacobsen who is equally appreciated for the furniture he designed as for his architecture, because Intentionallies has no intention of conforming to the contemporary role of the designer or the architect. The firm claims to be equally confident with projects sized 0.00008747m³ (a cell phone) as with buildings of 734,609m³ (Farglory U-Town). Just like Arne Jacobsen in his time, Intentionallies has the will to do everything. There is something slightly revolutionary about that ambition.

Daniel Golling

Editor in chief of *Forum magazine*

When I heard Shuwa Tei utter the name Yoshinobu Ashihara, I was able to understand instantly what Tei had been doing and he was going to do. I experience moments like this from time to time. Yoshinobu Ashihara was not only an architect who represented post-war modernism but also an excellent and unique educator. He had established the Department of Architecture at Musashino Art University where Tei studied. Ashihara later went on to teach at the University of Tokyo and became my beloved mentor. There are a few architects whom I call mentors, and Yoshinobu Ashihara is particularly special among them. That 'something' that I learned from him still lives on in me and keeps me going. That same 'something' undoubtedly lives inside Tei, and it will continue to keep him going. The moment I realized that, Tei became closer to me. I could see Professor Ahihara standing behind Tei.

What Ashihara tried to teach young students was, in essence, to remove boundaries. The world of architecture may seem liberal, but, in reality, it is segmented rigidly by various boundaries. For instance, there is a boundary between business and art. Developers focus only on business, causing architecture to become poor in quality, while architects see buildings only as art forms and scatter bulky concrete trash-like architecture all over the world.

Ashihara taught us how the city would become richer, more enjoyable and beautiful once the boundary between business and art disappeared, making the world of architecture better ventilated. With that in mind, Ashihara told us 'how to undertake projects' with enjoyable episodes he had encountered in his design studios. According to him, offers made in the morning tended not to work out, as people were likely at that time to be irritated. Evening was by far the best time when it came to making important requests. Young students, who thought that architectural design was a sacred and noble artistic endeavour, were stunned to hear such a story.

What Tei did with Hotel Claska was precisely what Ashihara had taught: Tei removed the boundary between business and art. Neither the world of business nor the world of art could not break away from their own frames, so they both remained inflexible. This is why there were no hotels in Tokyo to attract discerning people to stay. Hotel Claska provided a new business model that saved the hotels in Tokyo by removing the boundary between business and art. I wish I could have shown it to Ashihara and let him stay there.

In addition to the boundary between business and art, Ashihara sought to remove the boundary between daily life and architecture. Architecture naturally exists for daily life, so it is rather odd that there is this boundary between daily life and architecture. However, architecture often forgets about daily life and evolves in a malformed way into the world and is completely separate from it. Classicism and baroque were both the products of such an evolution, while 20th century modernism, too, attempted to reach the summit of a strange concept of aesthetics.

In Japan, Kenzo Tange (1913 - 2005) chose to pursue aesthetics in the same way as first generation modernism. Ashihara (1918 - 2003), however, did not follow suit. On the contrary, his theme was how to return to daily life. Ashihara was always cheerful and animated, but he also seemed somewhat solitary. This was particularly true because the generation that followed him, led by Isozaki or Kurokawa, once again pressed on, without referring to daily life, to explore grand, yet vain issues that were barely relevant to people. Their major proposition was that architecture was unbelievably beautiful on its own.

Where does Ashihara's stance stand in the history of modernism? Ashihara organized the history of modernism by saying that Alvar Aalto of Finland (1898 - 1976) revived the point of view of daily life in designs after Le Corbusier and Mies exhibited a type of 'violence'. This might have been due to the influence from Marcel Breuer (1902 – 1981), under whom he studied abroad at Harvard. Following the German rationalism of Walter Gropius (1883 – 1969), who laid the foundation of the Department of Architecture at Harvard, Breuer introduced a type of humanism into Harvard. Rather than a Gropius-style flat roof, Breuer preferred a pitched roof with a gentle gradient. Breuer skilfully slipped natural elements such as stones and trees into modernism in place of the massive blocks adopted by Gropius, who had been dubbed the 'Prince of Iron'.

Breuer was born in Hungary, a place that could be considered a connecting node (as their names are written with the last name first and first name last, as in Japan). His place of origin, I believe, had something to do with his humanism. Breuer played the role of a critic against modernism, just as Moholy-Nagy, also from Hungary, was critical of the Bauhaus movement.

I somehow feel the same slightly off-centred, humorous and warm feel from Tei's designs that Moholy-Nagy and Breuer's designs produce. Moholy-Nagy was on one side of the dichotomy, with Mies and Gropius on the other at the Bauhaus. Breuer was there to counter Gropius at Harvard, and Ashihara was at the opposite end of the spectrum from Kenzo Tange at the University of Tokyo. Ashihara's stance was succeeded by a handful of architects such as Mayumi Miyawaki and others who were called residence designers. However, even that lineage was severed by Tadao Ando's 'pure aesthetics', and the connection to the daily life was lost once again. The daily life advocates were surprisingly fragile.

Anyone who visited Ashihara's residence in the residential area in Yoyogi Uehara found a small wooden house and was surprised by its modesty and frugality. The architecture was surprisingly taciturn. I even wondered if this truly was the primary residence of such a great architect. Small items used in daily life and the greenery in the garden made a lively impression however, and welcomed visitors unceremoniously but courteously.

The items that Tei has designed give us the same impression as the items placed in Ashihara's house. Everything is seamless and welcoming in a familiar way. This is why they are finely designed but somewhat familiar at the same time. This, I believe, proves that familiarity is most needed in the 21th century.

It was the ultimate goal of designs in the 20th century to compete and excel in its sectionalist, tough-minded, individual fields. It was not only the social system but also the world of design that were compartmentalized. We are already aware that the winners of such competitions can never make people happy. By eliminating the boundaries, the world of design may be able to become one with daily life once again. We may be able to regain the true meaning of design for the sake of happiness. Tei's design provides such ideas for our time. This further provides many clues as to what role Japan could play as a critic of modern architecture and the world of design, just as East Europe and Scandinavia played critical roles in influencing the German and French mainstream in the early part of modernism.

Kengo Kuma

Founder of Kengo Kuma & Associates

INTENTIONALLIES
SHAPING *JAPAN* AND BEYOND

INDEX

p.137 Toy's Factory 1 | 1996
category: office
location: Shibuya, Tokyo
floor area: 300m²

p.138 Toy's Factory 2 | 1997
category: office
location: Shibuya, Tokyo
floor area: 450m²

p.139-140 Toy's Factory 3 | 1998
category: office
location: Shibuya, Tokyo
floor area: 210m²

p.141-143 Toy's Factory 4 | 2006
category: office
location: Shibuya, Tokyo
floor area: 450m²

p.144-145 Dance Music Record | 1999
category: record store
location: Shibuya, Tokyo
floor area: 600m²

p.146 Apollo | 1996
category: club
location: Aoyama, Tokyo
floor area: 210m²

p.147-149 Lounge O | 2004
category: bar
location: Aoyama, Tokyo
floor area: 231m²

p.150-151 Prime Sound Studio FORM | 2002
category: sound studio
location: Shibuya, Tokyo
floor area: 600m²

p.152 Ecru Sannomiya | 1999
category: retail store
location: Sannomiya, Kobe
floor area: 600m²

p.152 Ecru Venus Fort | 1999
category: retail store
location: Odaiba, Tokyo
floor area: 600m²

p .153 Dailies | 1998
category: retail store
location: Mitaka, Tokyo
floor area: 150m²

p.154-155 WA Shanghai | 2004
category: fashion building
location: Shanghai, China
floor area: 2000m²

p.156-157 Palette Plaza | 2007
category: retail store
location: Isezaki, Gunma
floor area: 60m²

p.158 JINS Kichijoji | 2006
category: retail store
location: Kichijoji, Tokyo
floor area: 87m²

p.159 LUXE DESIGN Maebashi | 2007
category: retail store
location: Maebashi, Gunma
floor area: 158m²

p.159 JINS Kamoi | 2007
category: retail store
location: Kamoi, Kanagawa
floor area: 83m²

p.159 JINS Hanyu | 2007
category: retail store
location: Hanyu, Saitama
floor area: 240m²

p.159 JINS Kagamihara | 2007
category: retail store
location: Kagamihara, GIfu
floor area: 180m²

p.160 JINS Senshu | 2007
category: retail store
location: Nagaoka, Niigata
floor area: 180m²

p.161 JINS Koshigaya | 2008
category: retail store
location: Koshigaya, Saitama
floor area: 274m²

p.161 JINS Niigata | 2007
category: retail store
location: Niigata
floor area: 240m²

p.161 JINS Morioka | 2008
category: retail store
location: Morioka, Iwate
floor area: 90m²

p.162-163 YEVS Koshigaya | 2008
category: retail store
location: Koshigaya, Saitama
floor area: 268.08m²

p.162-163 YEVS Shinjuku | 2009
category: retail store
location: Shinjuku, Tokyo
floor area: 210m²

p.164 United Arrows Ikebukuro | 2000
category: retail store
location: Ikebukuro, Tokyo
floor area: 600m²

p.165 United Arrows Nagoya | 2000
category: retail store
location: Nagoya, Aichi
floor area: 360m²

p.166 United Arrows DISTRICT | 2000
category: retail store
location: Shibuya, Tokyo
floor area: 210m²

p.169-177 Hotel Claska | 2003
category: hotel
location: Meguro, Tokyo
structure: RC
site area: 165m²
building area: 544m²
floor area: 3,114m²
(B1: 170m²/2F: 394m²/3F: 33m²/4F-5F: 507m²/6F: 287m²)

p.178-183 Jingumae Residence | 2006
category: office/residence
location: Jingumae, Tokyo
structure: RC
site area: 315m²
building area: 89m²
floor area: 496m²

p.184-187 Holland Hills | 2004
category: residence
location: Roppongi, Tokyo
floor area: 420m²

p.188-193 Marui Field | 2004
category: retail store
location: Shinjuku, Tokyo
floor area: 1,500m²

p.194-197 AGITO | 2003
category: retail store
location: Roppongi, Tokyo
floor area: 1500m²

p.198-203 United Cinema Toyosu | 2006
category: cinema complex
location: Toyosu, Tokyo
floor area: 6,987m²

p.204-207 Brillia Tower Osaki | 2006
category: residence
location: Shinagawa, Tokyo
structure: RC
site area: 3,169m²
building area: 984m²
floor area: 26,373m²
architecture design: Obayashigumi
developer: Tokyo Tatemono

p.208-213 Shibaura Bloom Tower | 2008
category: residence
location: Shibaura, Tokyo
site area: 13,847m²
building area: 4,669m²
floor area: 97,046m²
architecture design: Shimizu Corporation
developer: Mitsui Fudosan
           and Ken Corporation

p.214-215 Hangzhou resort | 2007
category: resort
location: Hangzhou, China
structure: RC
site area: 21,000m²
building area: 892 m²
floor area: 2,510m²

p.216-217 Minakami resort | 2007
category: resort
location: Minakami, Gunma
structure: RC
site area : 15,272m²
building area: 3,530m²
floor area: 4,960m²

p.218 Echord | 2006
category: proposal for resorts

p.219-225 W-residence | 2005
category: villa
location: Negara, Bali
structure: RC
site area: 5,707m²
building area: 892m²
floor area: 1,059m²
(Master Villa: 179m²/Ocean Front Villa: 80m²/
Garden Villa: 112m²)

p.228-239 ITL Villa | 2010
category: villa
location: Negara, Bali
structure: RC
site area: 8,405m²
building area: 2,346m²
floor area: 3,570m²
(Master Villa: 602m²/Ocean Front Villa: 412m²/
Garden Villa: 642m²/Pool Villa: 180m²)

p.240-249 SGM Villa | 2010
category: villa
location: Negara, Bali
structure: RC
site area: 12,650m²
building area: 2,889m²
floor area: 3,945m²

p.251 & 255 Ocean Front villa | concept
category: villa
location: Negara, Bali
site area: 9,100m²
building area: 1,500m²
floor area: 2,110m²

p.252 & 256 Lagoon villa | concept
category: villa
location: Negara, Bali
site area: 13,800m²
building area: 1,800m²
floor area: 2,400m²

p.253 & 257 ITL Lagoon villa | concept
category: villa
location: Negara, Bali
site area: 8,980m²
building area: 1,543m²
floor area: 1,835m²

p.259 JUT Taipei | 2011
category: residence
location: Taipei, Taiwan
structure: RC
site area: 5,360m²
building area: 1,100m²
floor area: 11,900m²

p.260-263 Farglory U-Town | 2014
category: retail store / office / museum
location: Taipei, Taiwan
structure: RC
site area: 46,280m²
building area: 23,198m²
floor area: 734,609m²

p.264-267 Farglory Taipei Dome | 2016
category: hotel / office / retail store /
           stadium
location: Taipei, Taiwan
structure: RC
site area : 102,500m²
floor area: 165,000m²

p. 268-271 Post Schematic City | concept
category: city planning
location: Tokyo
site area: 530,000m²
m&e: building facility design

Special thanks to

Aaron Lee, Akihiko Sato / Office Crane, Akihiro Nishimoto / LINC, Akinori Ban & Bun, Akira Aoyama, Akira Suzuki / A.S.A, APP China, Arisa Ono, Atsushi Ejiri, Atsushi Matsunaga / Ohkita medical clinic, Atsumi Hayashi, Azzami & Kunihiro Miyagi, Brooke Hodge, Bus Stop, Choi Eim Sik, Chao Teng-Hsiung, Cornelius, Craft Design Technology, Daniel Golling, David Marquardt, Monika Sandmayr / mach, Dramcan&dp, Edward Ryu / L.I.U Work Link, Emile Yamano, Hisao Takeda / Yamano and Associates, Endo Family, Eun-joo YANG, HWANG HYUN SUN, Yang-woo LEE / YOOshin, Fiona Wilson, Fumio Takashima, Hiroshi Nakiri / BALS, Haruomi Hosono, Hidenori Seki, Hirofumi Kiyonaga / soph., Hirokazu Okamoto, Hiromichi Tabata / TOTO, Hiromitsu Watanabe / DAA production, Hiroshi Kan, Hiroshi Kumamoto and Masaki Tabei and Realfleet, Hisaou Wakaizumi / Avex Marketing, Hisato Shiota, Kumiko Shiota / ERECTROGIC, Hitoshi Miyata, Hitoshi Tanaka and JINS staff / JINS, Hiroshi Okamoto / DMR, HMA Architects & Designers, Hoshikame Chair Factory, Hotel Claska, Huang Yu Chun & Zeng Zhen, Hur Seung Hyo, Iku Hirose, Isao Ichinose, Jun Aoki, Jun Saito, Junji Morishima, Kazuki Zenta / Yu-shin creation, Junji Tajima / Lidea, Junko Koyama, Kaori Miyawaki, Katsu Umebayashi / F.O.B.A, Katsuya Shirato, Katuhisa Kawai / Tokyo Tatemono, Kei Kobayashi & routine, Ken Kinoshita / RaNa design associates, inc., Kengo Kuma, Kenshi Uchinuno, Kim Gym, Kiyofumi Ohta, Koichi Inaba / Toy's Factory, Koji Tamura & Kazuya Omae, Kunihisa Akiyama / United Cinema, Lee Young Hye, Manabu Nagayama, Marbo / Lowrider, Mark F. Bedingham / Moët Hennessy ASIA PACIFIC, Masamichi Katayama / Wonderwall, Masanobu Sugatsuke / Sugatsuke Office, Masao Asaoka, Masaya Takeda / Mogreen, Masayuki Kuramochi, Michiko Wake, Michinobu Nonomura / AURA, Mika Yoshida, Mikiko Endo, Mikiko Manaka, Mineo Sakata, Mitsuhisa Sankyu Oiwa / Oring, Mitsuo Shindo / C.T.P.P., Mituru Sawada, Naoki Yamazaki / UP-FRONT GROUP, Naoki Watanabe, Naomi Hirabayashi / Plug-in Graphic, Norio Azuma, Sachiko Azuma / Sugar Matrix, Nicoletta Pedano, Nobuo Arakawa, Noriyuki Yano, Nousaku, Osamu Shigematsu / United Arrows, Pamera Mullinger, Patrick Lin, Poppy Shibamoto, Richard Spenser Powell, Robby Yung and Yin, Rose Percy, RUMIKO, Ryuichi Sakamoto, Sadahiro Nakamura, Hikaru Patric Okada / Transit General Office, Sakurai, SAMSUNG ELECTRONICS, Sanekazu Igari, Satoshi Uchihara / UCLD, Saul Taylor, Shibaura Tower | Mitsuifudosan / Shinnittetsu Toshikaihatsu / Ken corporation / Shimizu kensetu / Cassina ixc, Shin Takamatu, Shinji Abe, Shuya Okino & the Room, Starwood Hotels and Resorts Worldwide, Steve Teruggi, Stuart Daly, Susumu Sasaki / JUN, Suzukou Soubi, Takaaki Yamamoto, Takahito Noguchi / Dynamite Brothers Syndicate, Takashi Miki, Narutada Ootake/ Tokyu Corporation, Takatoshi Maruo / PT. Pasti Indah Indonesia Baru, Takeharu Sato, Takeshi Nacasa / Nacasa & Partners, Takeshi Natsuno, Takeyuki Gaino, Tei Kenchiku Kenkyujyo, Teijiro Handa, TGB Graphic, Tomohiko Sato, Tomoko Yamamoto, Toru Dodo, Toru Shimada, Toshikazu Tamaki, Toshiyuki Kita, Toshiyuki Sai, Towa Tei, Tycoon Graphics, Tyler Brûlé / Winkreative, TYMOTE, Weng Yongbiao, World , Yasuhiro Oshima / Plaza Create, Yasukazu Nishihata and Ary / Nakara Bali, Yasumasa Yokohama, Yasumichi Morita, Yasushi Fujimoto / CAP, Yoshiaki Nagai / R investment & design, Yoshihiro Saito / A-study, Yoshiko Yoneyama, Yoshitsugu Takagi, Yudai Tachikawa / t.c.k.w, Yugo Nakamura, Yukihiro Takahashi, Yukio Arita / NEC, Yutaka Kinoshita, Yutanpo Shirane, Zhu Changning, Fu Yi Jing, Liu Xing Rong

Photo Credit

Dan Tobin Smith(017-019), Intentionallies(058, 084, 090, 125, 178), Kazunari Tajima(038), Kiyonori Okuyama(028-033), Koji Fujii / Nacasa & Partners Inc.(078), Kei Takashima / Nacasa & Partners Inc.(129_Nanba), Mineo Sakata(057, 059-061, 067-069, 084-087, 092-093, 098-099, 102-105, 111-115, 126, 134-135, 137-140, 144-146, 152-153, 164-166, 194-197), Ralf Barthelmes(079), Realfleet(021, 023, 025, 034-037, 039-042, 044-055), Satoshi Minakawa(169), Seishi Maeda(089), Shinichi Ito(106-107), Takeshi Nakasa / Nacasa & Partners Inc.(209, 213 bottom), Toshiyuki Yano / Nacasa & Partners Inc.(064-065, 070-071, 077, 080-083, 091, 094-097, 100-101, 108-109, 117-124, 127, 130-133, 141-143, 147-151, 154-163, 170-177, 179-183, 184-193, 198-208, 210-212, 213 middle and top, 218-219, 222-225), Toshiyuki Yano(072-075, 228-229, 231-232, 234-241, 243-245, 248-249), Tsukuru Asada(063), Yuko Iitoyo(027, 043)

Illustration

Hiroshi kan(220-221, 226-227, 230-231, 233, 236, 242, 246-247)
Mo-Green(268-271)

 **INTENTIONALLIES**

Jingumae Residence. 3-40-9 Jingumae
Shibuya-ku, Tokyo 150-0001 JAPAN
tel: 03.5786.1084 / fax: 03.5786.1453

www.intentionallies.co.jp/
post@intentionallies.co.jp

Chairman:
Shuwa Tei
Keiko Katori

Member:
Norio Unno
Tomofumi Shimoda
Kenji Nagai
Tetsushi Iwata
Kei Sagara
Keigo Masuda
Yoshiaki Furuya (external accounting)
Naoto Nakamura (in Stockholm)

Staff:
Yukari Hirose
Mayumi Okano
Kayo Sugawara (in Bali)

Founder:
Shuwa Tei
Shin Ohori
Jiro Endo

 **TycoonGraphics**

Villa Gloria #602. 2-31-7 Jingumae
Shibuya-ku, Tokyo 150-0001 JAPAN
tel: 03.5411.5341 / fax: 03.5411.5342

http://www.tycoon.jp/
mail@tycoon.jp

INTENTIONALLIES
SHAPING *JAPAN* AND BEYOND

Publisher
Frame Publishers

Production
Marlous van Rossum-Willems and Naoto Nakamura

Author
Shuwa Tei

Graphic design
Tycoon Graphics

Translation
Yurika Araki Dennis, Kazuya Nakagawa and Naoto Nakamura

Copy editing
Charlotte Vaudrey

Prepress
Edward de Nijs
Neroc.nu

Printing
DPrint, Singapore

Trade distribution USA and Canada
Consortium Book Sales & Distribution, LLC.
34 Thirteenth Avenue NE, Suite 101
Minneapolis, MN 55413-1007
T +1 612 746 2600
T +1 800 283 3572 (orders)
F +1 612 746 2606

Distribution rest of world
Frame Publishers
Laan der Hesperiden 68
1076 DX Amsterdam
The Netherlands
www.framemag.com
distribution@framemag.com

ISBN: 978-90-77174-34-0

© 2011 Frame Publishers, Amsterdam, 2011